HYPERTHINKING

hyperthinking *n* a radical philosophical discipline *and* practical thinking process that advocates ongoing intellectual adaptation and development to meet the changes imposed by a rapidly moving, Internet-driven age. Used especially in business and commercial contexts. See also definitions of its four constituent dimensions: **hypershifting**; **hyperlearning**; **hyperlinking**; and **hyperacting**

hyperthinker *n* one who engages in the practice of hyperthinking

hyperthink *vb* (*intr*) **hyperthinks, hyperthinking, hyperthought** to engage in the practice of hyperthinking (either consciously or unconsciously) by adopting the specific set of intellectual tools and thinking techniques set forth in that philosophy

For more on hyperthinking, visit

www www.hyperthinking.net

www www.hyperthinker.com

www www.zn.be

f www.facebook.com/hyperthinker

www.twitter.com/hyperthinker

HyperThinking

Creating a New Mindset for the
Age of Networks

Philip Weiss

GOWER

Published by
Gower Publishing Limited
Wey Court East
Union Road
Farnham
Surrey GU9 7PT
England

Gower Publishing Company
Suite 420
101 Cherry Street
Burlington, VT 05401-4405
USA

www.gowerpublishing.com

British Library Cataloguing in Publication Data
Weiss, Philip.
  Hyperthinking : creating a new mindset for the age of
  networks.
  1. Management--Psychological aspects. 2. Management--
  Technological innovations. 3. Business--Technological
  innovations.
  I. Title
  658.4'0019-dc23

ISBN 978-1-4094-2845-9 (pbk)
ISBN 978-1-4094-2846-6 (ebk – PDF)
ISBN 978-1-4094-8456-1 (ebk – ePUB)

Library of Congress Cataloging-in-Publication Data
Weiss, Philip.
  Hyperthinking : creating a new mindset for the age of networks / by Philip
Weiss.
     p. cm.
  Includes bibliographical references and index.
  ISBN 978-1-4094-2845-9 (pbk) -- ISBN 978-1-4094-2846-6 (ebk)
1. Information technology--Management. 2. Technological innovations--
Management. 3. Internet--Social aspects. 4. Change (Psychology)
5. Organizational change. 6. Management--Social aspects. I. Title.
  HD30.2.W4525 2012
  658.4'038--dc23

2012022758

Printed and bound in Great Britain by the
MPG Books Group, UK

Contents

Reviews for HyperThinking: Creating a New Mindset for the Age of Networks

Networks don't just change the way we interact with each other; they change the way we think, we learn and how we make decisions. Philip Weiss' HyperThinking *captures the essence of these changes convincingly and provides you with a clear route to the thinking processes you will need to survive and thrive in this radically new and fast-changing business environment.*

Thomas Power, CEO and founder Ecademy

Shifting your thinking patterns is the key to embracing change. HyperThinking *is the kind of book you should read when you are in the middle of change, of a conflict, when you're managing a difficult project, when you just changed jobs, when you had your first child, when you just retired. It's a book about the way we think, or rather the way we think we think, and what this means for the rest of our lives. What this book taught me is that we have to live in a world where we cannot rely on traditional thinking patterns – these must be continuously challenged if we want to adapt to the ever-changing environment we live in. This is called hyperthinking, and it is giving people who want to make an impact on the world we live in a competitive edge. Some are natural-born hyperthinkers, others will have to learn it the hard way. This book will give you a headstart and will provide for an enjoyable and thought-provoking read. I'm proud to be a hyperthinker. Soon, you will feel the same way too.*

Aurélie Valtat, Digital Communications Manager,
European Council

HyperThinking *reminds us that we live in a constant flux of ideas and events, propelled along by the economics, technology and politics of our time. But Phil Weiss takes us beyond Heraclitus as he explores the tools for navigating the ever-changing river. By embracing the four modes of hyperthinking, everyone can move beyond convention and the fear of failure, and flex their thinking-muscles for innovative outcomes. In spite of the proven results over 100 years of the Montessoris and Steiners and Neills and Piagets of this world, most national education systems still turn out far more conformists than iconoclasts – possibly a good thing for the stability of society, but not for stimulating life-long creative learning. With* HyperThinking, *Phil Weiss shows how to shed sluggish groupthink and apply heuristic playfulness to your workday – or even personal – problems. How to leave behind the conservatism of traditional formal education and shift to more creative solutions by enthusiastically engaging technology in networking and learning. Read this book before a hyperthinker makes your job irrelevant!*

Ian Andersen, External Communications Adviser,
European Commission

Phil Weiss invented the concept of hyperthinking. In these pages he brings his ideas alive and shares the principles with a flair for storytelling and an eclectic mix of sources, examples and case studies. He's the Tony Buzan of the Internet generation.

Marc Wright, Chairman, simplygroup

Change – be it cultural, social or economic – seems to have hit hyperspeed as technology facilitates ever faster and easier social networking. Weiss takes a long, unblinking look at this world in constant flux, and sees only promise and opportunity. His hyperthinking approach gives readers a practical and structured way to embrace change, incorporate it into their lives, and thrive in the wild, wired west.

Drawing upon great thinkers like Nieztche, Thomas Kuhn, Nassim Nicholas Taleb, and his own experiences and those of others, Weiss proposes a 4-dimensional hyper-approach. First, detachment allows yourself to see how you think, and to recognize the paradigms within which our thinking may stagnate. Then, to escape our calcified mental models we need to adopt a state of permanent learning. Playful exploration of the web and social media, allows us to connect, share and expand the reach and impact of our actions. And finally, quite simply, we are told to experiment, to act, to get out there and make things happen.

Weiss demystifies the digital world and provides simple and practical advice on how to thrive in the new wired society.
Angus Thomson, Director, Vaccination
Policy & Advocacy, Sanofi Pasteur

Innovation will come from people and entities who understand networks, and recognize new types of intelligence in those networks. This world of exponential innovation, in which everything is connecting to everything else, will need more hyperthinkers.
Samia Lounis De Brouwer, Co-Founder Scanadu
and Director TEDxBrussels

Philip Weiss is one of the most creative thinkers of his generation. Straight from Oxford he founded the ZN agency, which engaged major global corporations from the dawn of the internet age.

HyperThinking *is a distillation of his experience at ZN, and provokes us all to benefit from the family of internet technologies, in the way we handle life and work in a rapidly changing world. Profound as well as playful,* HyperThinking *invites us all to immerse ourselves in the new technologies – and adapt our analysis, thinking and behaviour for the networked world. An important book for all those involved in communicating ideas, policies and activities for their business.*

James Arnold-Baker, former CEO Oxford University Press, founding Chairman of Doctors.net.uk

Acknowledgements

The people who have inspired and helped me to write this book, and more importantly to define the concept of hyperthinking, are too numerous to mention here. However, I would like to acknowledge someone who has always inspired me with the confidence and willingness to follow my own ideas, and who helped me overcome some of the writer's block that inevitably seems to accompany this kind of endeavour: my mother. She has always had more faith in me than I did myself, and this has given me the confidence to venture into the unknown more than once.

I want to thank my family who had to endure me, over several years, explaining time and again new and strange words, and walking around in circles trying to get the book under way.

A special and deep appreciation goes to my wife, Ramola, who has followed me from the sunny skies of India to the grey ones of Brussels, and has had to 'hypershift' many times to get used to her new home; through her boundless enthusiasm and positive energy she has shown me how to adapt and thrive.

Ivan, my son, and Natasha, my daughter, have both been relentless – in the best possible way – teachers of what it is like to have a 'soft paradigm' and embrace new skills, new ideas and new technology without the slightest apprehension.

Through our travels together and our endless discussions, I learn from them everyday.

And finally, my colleagues at ZN, who have helped me to clarify and put into practice the concepts outlined in this book; they challenge me daily on how useful and relevant these concepts are to their work, and they have all helped shape the ideas as they exist today.

I also owe a debt of gratitude to my clients and those who I have described in this book as 'hyperthinkers'; whether or not they are aware of the word, they have inspired me to articulate this new concept and 'try it out' in the real world.

Special thanks goes to my publisher Jonathan Norman, who believed that there was a potential audience for yet another new word to add to the overburdened business executive, and to Andrew Lewis for helping me get the words and the flow of the book into the shape they are in today.

Hyperthinking: Executive Summary

Hyperthinking in action is as easy as it is powerful; understanding the concepts that underpin the theory, however, is not so simple. To help you get to grips with the essence and flow of my ideas, and thus begin your hyperthinking journey, this book has been divided into five distinct parts.

In Part One we meet the three main characters: Aurélie, Paul and yourself. We begin with Aurélie who, while working for a large and complex organisation in the midst of an unparalleled crisis, was able to use technological tools that are often derided as frivolous toys in an innovative and practical way. In so doing she achieved remarkable personal success. We then use her experiences to help us assess the way we ourselves operate, enabling us to see how 'the rules of the game' have changed and what this means for us as individuals.

Next we meet Paul, a fictional character who we accompany on a journey that will almost certainly echo the recent experiences of many people working in business as well as many other professions. Paul's story begins with a painful encounter at work, daunting challenges and new technology, and quickly leads him to the distinct feeling that 'business as usual' is a phrase that should be committed to the history books.

In Part Two we step back in time to my undergraduate days at Oxford studying philosophy, politics and economics. That was where I first encountered the concepts of shifting paradigms and perspectivism, ideas which help us to perceive reality from alternative vantage points. This part of the book contains the conceptual foundations that are required if we are to shift perspectives and create new versions of reality. These principles are built upon by the power of a single word, a word which enables us to not only think differently but also to develop new skills. These chapters represent the core rationale behind hyperthinking.

In Part Three we examine in detail the four dimensions of hyperthinking. These dimensions give the conceptual model an actionable structure; they facilitate a more fluid mindset that happily embraces change, creativity and technology. This section is divided between the four dimensions of hyperthinking and is followed by a chapter in which I consider how it can be applied to teams to create new forms of collaboration. The four dimensions are:

- Hypershift – the notion that we need to understand our existing paradigms and learn to alter our perceptions.

- Hyperlearn – combining continuous learning and experimentation, thus sharpening our mental skills.

- Hyperlink – something that reminds us of the vital importance of new technologies and the fact that, however comfortable they make us feel, it is mandatory to embrace and use them in every aspect of our lives. Doing this will expand our reach and impact.

- Hyperact – the final dimension that stresses the importance of execution and the challenges we face when coming up with new ideas that rely on technology. It is the ability to conceive, prototype and test ideas to determine their usefulness.

In Part Four we turn to the practical application of hyperthinking and introduce the four dimensions to daily life. We look at ways to turn mere concepts into actual habits and adapt them to our own personal circumstances. We look at examples that will enable anyone to start hyperthinking straight away.

And in Part Five, the final part of the book, we look at some real practitioners who have – without necessarily knowing it – applied hyperthinking to a variety of different projects. We see how, by unconsciously following the assumptions set out in this book, they were able to reinvent reality, get results and ultimately reach their goals.

To conclude, we catch up with Paul and see how he completes his journey.

PART ONE

The Beginning of the End of Business as Usual

① Flying High

When Aurélie Valtat woke up on the morning of 15 April 2010 she had no idea that an obscure volcano in Iceland was about to bring great swathes of the skies above the western world, and beyond, to a grinding halt. Mount Eyjafjallajökull in Iceland had erupted violently the previous evening, sending a vast cloud of smoke and ash high into the air. Prevailing and, to the people affected, seemingly malign winds did the rest and the plumes of ash were soon streaming south towards Europe. By midday the UK had banned all except emergency flights, and other countries soon followed suit, closing off large swathes of European airspace. Suddenly, and largely without warning, business travel and holidays, aspects of life that we have come to take for granted, were no longer a given. Mount Eyjafjallajökull had started a crisis that would eventually disrupt the travel plans of 9 million people around the world, with over 100,000 flights cancelled and 77 per cent of European airspace closed. The timing could not have been worse as many people were enjoying an overseas Easter break; and as the news spread, stranded passengers started to wonder how they would ever get back home. Those who could turn to the Internet for information went first to airline sites, then to general news sites and finally to Eurocontrol, the large civil-military intergovernmental organisation that coordinates air traffic management across 39 countries. However, nowhere could they find the information they were seeking. Online communications manager Aurélie quickly realised that updates to the Eurocontrol website were taking far too long to satisfy an understandably impatient public, so she decided to make information available more rapidly by using social media networks.

Over the next few days the Eurocontrol Twitter feed went from a few hundred to thousands of followers, many of whom were asking for urgent help and advice. The organisation had no established procedures to deal with the questions that were now flooding in on Twitter, so Aurélie did what she thought made sense: she improvised. Luckily she speaks four languages – including Chinese – and is a closet geek, happy to quietly play around with new technology when others are busy writing procedural reports and other vital documents. Without any guidelines at all she decided to follow the adage 'better to ask forgiveness than permission', and so she started to engage with the people asking questions on Twitter. But she did not just engage in the bland and neutral way that company spokespersons usually do: she offered people the most precious commodity that, in the circumstances, she had – relevant information to help them find a way home.

Just as the ash cloud was beginning to do its worst I was starting to head home to Brussels after a short holiday in Thailand. As I was waiting for my flight I casually updated my status on Twitter. A few minutes after writing 'About to board the flight to Brussels' I received a reply: 'Don't count on it. Airports are being closed down in Brussels and around Europe'. The message was from Aurélie at Eurocontrol; she was connected to me on my LinkedIn profile as we had been in contact on a few occasions and was part of my social network of 'friends' – people you know 'virtually' better than you do face to face. I was a little sceptical of her message at first as the departures board in front of me suggested that we were just minutes away from boarding the flight. However, just as our luggage was on the verge of being loaded the board suddenly changed completely to display all flights to European destinations as cancelled. I looked at the counter clerk, who had obviously received no confirmatory instructions and was about to send my family's suitcases on a mysterious journey, and impulsively asked her to wait. Only a few minutes later she confirmed that the flight was not going to be leaving any time soon. Aurélie had been right! I was deeply impressed by the hidden power of the information networks that connected us: by being alerted some minutes before everyone else I had been able to act and save my luggage. Over the next few days I – along with thousands of others around the world – assiduously checked Eurocontrol and Aurélie's Twitter accounts looking for any hint of when flights would resume.

Thus it was that I personally became one of Aurélie's numerous Twitter followers, and she now finds her story introducing this book. Her then employer, Eurocontrol, is no lean start-up firm, and nor is it a flexible company where you get a day a week to work on your dream project. It is not that the organisation's culture is unfriendly, but it is as rigid and complex as many similar institutions. Yet despite this, her actions convinced the powers that be that the Web and social media could be used to help the organisation do its job better, and Aurélie's improvisations during the ash cloud crisis have led to significant changes in the way that Eurocontrol manages public and press relations. And little wonder: her radical decision was fully vindicated by the fact that she was able to help scores of people, including some whom the situation threatened with genuine emotional anguish. She later remarked:

> *We saved at least three weddings. I was even proposed to! We had a direct message from a Spanish airline*

thanking us as they were getting information faster from our Twitter feed than from their own air traffic control.

In hindsight what Aurélie did throughout these events was truly heroic. The only colleague who could have helped her was himself stranded, but this mother of two young children maintained the interaction single-handedly, often for more than 16 hours a day, until air traffic returned to normal a week later. Aurélie's actions came completely naturally to her. She dealt with an unprecedented situation in her professional life by creatively applying a new technological tool, motivated by a fundamental belief in the urgent need we all have to communicate in an open and transparent way. That single, innovative decision transformed Aurélie's life: she quickly became a sought-after speaker on the social media circuit and has since been snapped up by the European Council to manage their online communications. Who knows what she will achieve next. Aurélie is not a unique figure; similar individuals in thousands of businesses and organisations are challenging the status quo every day. They are doing brilliant things using new technology and their innate creativity to change the world – or, perhaps more accurately, to change their *own* worlds. They do this because they feel emotionally compelled and driven to it. In this book I will endeavour to describe what it is that I believe makes people think differently and try new ways of doing things, and how this has changed – and will continue to change – the world, one hyperlink at a time. I will identify what these people have in common, and I will paint a picture of a radical new mindset that is emerging, one that is changing the way we work, live and learn. It is called hyperthinking, and it is about to change your world too.

② Risks or Opportunities?

I am fairly sure that the world does not want, or need, another author telling it at great length that business and technology – indeed the very fundamentals of human society – are undergoing dramatic changes. Legions of journalists, pundits, academics and bar-room philosophers have already done plenty to analyse, measure and quantify what is happening and then predict the outcomes. I wish them the best of luck with their efforts. Many people – including myself – shy away from contemplating these things at length. When we stop to consider the myriad possible implications of the huge shifts that we are experiencing, trying to make even basic sense of it all can lead to feelings of overwhelming confusion and, worse, hopelessness. We crave reassurance from some figure in authority that there is a way to understand what is going on, and when – as is so often the case – we are not given it we feel a debilitating sense of despair. I am convinced that this despondency is a widespread problem, and one that will have serious consequences unless we tackle it. Of course one cannot quantify it, and it *is* self-evidently mistaken in many respects, but there can be no doubt that there is a general sense of malaise out there, an ill-defined feeling that ours is a period afflicted by unique crises and that things are only going to get worse. The immense and far-reaching effects of technological progress are the most visible manifestations of the unsettling changes we have recently experienced, but to make matters worse the political and economic landscape seems equally convulsed by uncontrollable and menacing events:

- adverse shifts in the geo-political balance of power;

- financial problems that threaten to ruin the economy;

- a new and widespread fear of science, ecological collapse and environmental disaster;

- terrorists undermining the very fabric of our civilisation;

- a process of globalisation that has turned and now threatens to consume us …

Need I go on? If you want it to be, the list of intractable problems can seem endless; no wonder the gloom is palpable.

Perhaps part of the explanation for the uneasy sense of foreboding about our future prospects lies in the fact that our instincts seem to be designed to make us fear change deeply. Human nature appears to like stable, recognisable patterns and seems to want to predict the future – or at least to know that some basic truths today will remain the same tomorrow. But at all levels – personal, institutional and societal – and especially in a period of remorseless change, these instincts surely cannot continue to serve us well. In fact, an overly cautious approach to life in the modern world can be seen as deeply counter-productive to our well-being: the greater the change the greater our instinctive fear of it, and so the more we resist rather than actively seize the potential to take advantage of new situations as they arise, putting ourselves at a clear disadvantage as the world quickly moves on without us. There are innumerable examples of this retreat from the realities of modernity. We all know of anxious companies and their managers who are fearful of technology and aggressively seek to resist its advance; and consider the increasingly negative comments about Facebook, Google and Microsoft, and think how, for all the howling ferocity of the backlash, it does little more than illustrate that people's growing apprehension about these companies blinds them to the benefits and opportunities that they clearly offer.

It may be a hard truth to accept for many, but it is the truth that in our professional lives we now need to accept constant change and the fact that there is no longer job security of the sort that our parents enjoyed. Yet accepting this simple fact, and being more flexible in our responses, could be a way to actually increase our security. Being freelance, for example, although it might look more precarious than having a permanent job, can be a much less risky strategy in times of recession as firms will find it more attractive to contract out small projects to freelancers rather than retaining people on a full-time (and expensive) basis. So, paradoxically, what looks like a high-risk strategy might, in certain circumstances, end up being the safest bet; and yet how many people express horror at the very thought of becoming freelance? Our instincts constantly tell us to fear and minimise risk, but the excess of caution that this generates can lead to the very outcome that we wish to avoid. I have seen the process occur in business time and time again, inevitably with adverse effects. A company that is desperately trying to avoid trouble over a contentious issue might decide to keep quiet about it, afraid that by talking they will only draw attention to the problem. However, in the Internet age an organisation's silence can ensure that others will assume control of the issue, and by the time it is realised that a mistake has been made it is too late to react. In place of the convenient silence that was sought, a deafening and damaging controversy ensues. We saw this with the uproar over the H1N1 flu virus, when a great deal of fear and concern flowed over on the Internet. The authorities were slow to react and explain the benefits of vaccines; they remained on the back foot and the result was a needless – and indeed baseless – furore.

We in the twenty-first century are not unique in having this essentially pessimistic outlook. It is deeply rooted in European history and culture, so much so that one could argue that it almost forms a folk-memory that continues to condition our behaviour today. The first reaction to change throughout European history seems invariably to have been one of fear – institutional and personal. Look at the terrified response to the invention of the printing press in the fifteenth century: officials in the church – one of the dominant institutional powers at the time – reacted strongly against a perceived challenge to its monopoly of power and authority, and often visited terrible punishments upon those brave and radical beings who eagerly grasped the new technology. Or consider the Industrial Revolution and the spread of its numerous and (let's not forget, which we often do) beneficial achievements. The widely expressed fear that greeted the invention and spread of the telegraph has a distinctly familiar ring to modern ears. People strongly argued that the telegraph would lead to frenzy, information overload and an insane rhythm of life – arguments that with a little recasting might have been trotted out a few years ago by the pundits who bemoan and loudly decry, among other things, the latest technological innovations (although doubtless those very same hacks did not write their articles using pen and paper, preferring those handy PCs that they all happen to own). So, based on historical precedents, it was no surprise when the Internet initially generated a colossal amount of fear and loathing. And although that first wave of hostility may have been overcome, the nagging sense persists that for all the advantages we derive from this wonderful invention we have actually signed a Faustian pact, compromising our privacy, blurring our notions of good and bad, and – for good measure – destroying our ability to concentrate. It is yet another river of gloom feeding into the sea of despondency that we insist on creating for ourselves.

I do not underestimate the gravity of any of these issues, but nor do I wish to dwell on them for too long here. The arguments about the hows and the whys of all of these problems have been well aired many times elsewhere. Instead, I want to pose a radical question and ask what, in this challenging period, can we practically do to help ourselves live, and live *well* – both professionally and personally. And in that regard I believe that one thing each of us can do is, as Ian Andersen – an innovative European Union (EU) bureaucrat whom you will meet later in this book – once told me, to start finding the right questions to ask rather than the answers, although finding them would help of course. So the question I ask is simply this: is mentally retreating to the mythical good old days, where we rely on ever-cautious instinct, the right strategy for dealing with constant technological change and political uncertainty? Or should we finally move on and start believing that we have the collective ability as ingenious, free-thinking and creative individuals to solve these problems cumulatively through the imaginative application of technology? My own view is, of course, unequivocal: we must look dispassionately at our traditional instincts and decide whether or not they are relevant and actually useful to us. And if we do this and reach the conclusions that I think are self-evident, I believe that we will immediately see the benefits to be had when we learn to keep these negative and fearful instincts in check. If we understand that risk-taking – and even failure – does not always lead to unmitigated disaster but can be beneficial and even fun, we can start to embrace change – and not just embrace it but enjoy it for its own sake. Who knows – we may even finally come to terms with the fact that technology will help to save, not destroy us.

To western minds the fact that the Chinese character that means 'crisis' contains the signs for 'danger' *and* 'opportunity' is completely counter-intuitive, and yet I am convinced that it accurately captures the essence of something that we have been missing. We know that the world is full of dangers all right – we are reminded of the fact all the time – but it is also full of opportunities. It just needs the right sort of thinking to replace our deeply felt fears with new confidence. In short, we need to rethink completely how we view things, and, as I am certain is necessary and will explore later, shift our perspective. A new way of thinking is needed in order to enable us to use and productively apply the new modes of working that have developed around us so quickly. 'This is our time', said Sean Parker in the zeitgeist defining movie *The Social Network* (2010) – it is indeed, and I would add that we just need to understand it. Although the loud public debates about the issue of constant change and its effects will doubtless continue, the big and deceptively simple question will remain once the shouting dies down: what, if anything, can I actually do about all of this? It is to this ordinary but profound question that I hope to provide some answers during the course of this book, but first I want you to meet someone – although you may feel as though you have met him somewhere before.

③ Meet Paul

For Paul, a communications manager at Global World Corp, the start of a career in business had gone pretty well, and he had much to feel pleased about: he had attended a respected university, got a decent degree and had quickly landed a great job at a leading global company. He had worked in London for the first few years of his job, and had then transferred to the firm's European HQ in Brussels. At that point – slowly getting used to his newly adopted city – he still had no reason to doubt that his would be a smooth ride to the top of the business world. Ambitious, smart and articulate, Paul was confident and self-possessed enough to feel sure that he was ready to shoulder more responsibility for his employers. So at first all went according to plan, but then came the shockingly unexpected cataclysm of 9/11 and the savage recession that followed, events which plunged his world into turmoil. For a few months no one seemed to know what would happen next, and Paul's professional life was shaken by endless rumours and scare-stories. But eventually the smoke started to clear and things looked bright again. It did not last. Bang! The sub-prime crisis brought all the fear and uncertainty flooding back; and worse was to come, for by now Paul was beginning to wonder if he had a long-term future at the company, and even whether he wanted one. There had always been cost-cutting, but the brutal way in which the latest round had been implemented had been deeply disturbing for him. It seemed that there was no guaranteed place, even for loyal and hard-working individuals, in this new and unforgiving business environment. The very bedrock of his personal beliefs seemed to be eroding before his eyes.

Thus it was that some five years into his career Paul had begun to think that nothing around him was predictable any more. Every month seemed to bring bewildering changes, from revolutions in the Middle East to terrorist attacks and natural disasters. It all increased his profound feelings of uncertainty. And technology – the supposed great liberator of humankind from workplace drudgery – did not help; it merely continued on its inexorable forward march, deaf to his exasperated pleas for help and leaving him stranded far behind. First it was the Web, then e-commerce. At one point it was Second Life, then Facebook, LinkedIn, Twitter and even more increasingly obscure fads. Paul found it tough, if not impossible, to keep track of them all. It was now no longer a question of who had moved his Blackberry, but whether he was going to be forced into an iPhone and iPad apprenticeship. He knew only too well that the barriers between his personal and professional lives were dissolving and that he was now working more and more in the evenings and at weekends; but what was the truth of the matter? Everyone claimed as much, but had technology *really* changed the way to do business for the better. Did it actually matter? Paul was not in the technology sector, but he was beginning to feel as if he had been transferred there without being informed of the fact, because it felt as if *everyone* was in there now, like it or not. Secretly, Paul knew that he had been marooned by his own fear of rapid change and a wilful ignorance that had grown out of that fear, but he had convinced himself that it was too late to catch up now. His reaction to this self-imposed dilemma was to dismiss it all as loud and empty hype, and he had little patience with the techno-geeks at Global World Corp who seemed to get excited about everything that 'iShines'. Paul now found himself inwardly screaming much of the time: he knew that he *was* intelligent, but on most days he did not feel that way. He felt that the world had moved rapidly around and beyond him, but his mind could not begin to grasp what needed to be done in order to keep up.

To add to this existential angst, Paul was also worried about his more immediate future: the office had become tensely political and a deeply riven and unhappy place to work. And to his dismay Paul realised that most of his assets were firmly tied to his job, the company and his internal network. He was not short of 'friends' – but would they help him if he had to move to another company or, worse still, if he became a casualty of change? Paul sensed he was at a crossroads: he felt he had lost his mojo, and if he did not make some changes he believed that his career might take a turn for the worse. And there seemed to be no respite, no time to gather his thoughts and plan. 'This is the third time in the last six months', Paul muttered to himself as the invitation to a senior management strategy meeting landed in his in-box. He suspected that the 'important announcement setting out the new vision of the company' was simply code for yet another round of ineffective restructuring. Global World Corp was not having a happy recession. Two years earlier the chief executive officer (CEO) had been fired in a shareholder revolt. His successor had been unable to restore confidence in the company and had resigned after a year. An interim CEO was appointed, but so far the new board had not seemed able to take any decision other than that of bringing in expensive consultants to tell them which bits of the company should be cut back to save costs. Paul's own department had been badly knocked about by this wave of change. Although only a few of his colleagues had been fired, budgets were frozen then cut, and everyone now felt as if something very bad might be about to happen to them next. Paul had actually done well on a couple of recent projects, but such was his black mood that he usually arrived at the office wondering if that day would be his last. He *was* optimistic by nature and convinced that he was still managing to put on a good show, but Paul's enthusiasm and energy for his work was beginning to wear dangerously thin. Every move was being carefully watched at World Corp's global HQ in the US, where someone was surely busy dreaming up the next round of restructuring. And so, growing increasingly demoralised and depressed, Paul sat back and hoped and waited for things to get back to normal. His inertia could have been a serious mistake.

The incident that nearly proved to be Paul's undoing came out of the blue when the company found itself ensnared in a serious and acrimonious dispute: one of its leading products was being loudly criticised online. It had started with just a single disgruntled customer, but her wild claims (that she had been made ill by a chemical component in one of the company's products) were apparently gaining traction. This issue was the only item on the agenda for the late afternoon departmental meeting that Paul headed to with weary resignation.

Pamela, Paul's 38-year-old boss, appeared under enormous pressure as she rose from her desk to join the four middle-aged managers seated at the small conference table. She launched straight in:

> *This could become a major problem. There is no scientific basis to the accusations, but the rumours are spreading. Our retailers are getting nervous and the*

press wants an explanation. The statements we have issued about our rigorous testing only seem to have made things worse. Our unhappy customer seems to spend her entire time on this Facebook group attacking us, and she is being joined by dozens if not hundreds of others.

She turned to Paul and looked him straight in the eye:

Paul, I need you to figure out how we can stop this, turn it around and make sure this story does not do any damage to our sales, which frankly could not really be in worse shape at present.

Paul felt his heart sinking. He was not at all familiar with Facebook. He had heard about it, of course, and had even signed up when an old friend invited him to join, but he had rarely been back on the site. He had been raised to believe in the importance of privacy, and was thoroughly disconcerted to hear about his younger cousins using the site to upload ridiculous pictures of their nights of youthful debauchery, fearing that such public records would probably come back to bite them hard later in life. Like many of his colleagues and peers, Paul had dismissed Facebook as a trivial toy, fit only for sulky teenagers and easily distracted students; what possible place could it have in the serious world of business? Facebook was not, he had quickly decided, something that would prove very useful for him, and he had not been shy about making his opinions known to all who would listen. Oddly enough though, he had enjoyed the movie *The Social Network*, and it was perhaps in response to this guilty pleasure that he made sure afterwards to loudly proclaim that it had only increased his dislike for Facebook, and his suspicion that its founder, Mark Zuckerberg, was out to get him.

'Paul?' Pamela had paused, waiting for Paul to say something; the others were looking at him expectantly. At the same time that Paul became aware that he had drifted, he realised that he did not have the faintest idea of where to begin with this project. It was a sickening moment. 'Uh, ok, so what do you want me to do?' he ventured tentatively. 'Figure it out and come back to me with a plan by yesterday', Pamela snapped. 'If we do not do something quickly, we could all suffer the consequences'. Paul put on a brave face, smiled and acquiesced. He went home feeling irritated, tired and depressed.

First thing next morning, Paul dropped in on the IT department and explained his problem. The smirking youth he spoke to obviously sensed Paul's discomfort and gleefully said that access to Facebook on the company network had been stopped because it had proved such a distraction to people. He would need to look into this elsewhere; and with that the youth swivelled in his chair and waved Paul away. Desperate for a straw to clutch, Paul felt somehow vindicated that at least the IT team also saw the site as an irresistible diversion that needed to be banned. He only wished that there was a way to outlaw the damn thing entirely and ensure that it would not trouble anyone in his position again. Paul tried a couple of colleagues who worked on the corporate website, but they had little idea of how to help him. He searched the Web for information about online crisis management, but all he found were numerous grim stories of companies that had reacted too slowly and had ended up spending vast amounts of money on PR agencies and lawyers, only to look ridiculous in the end.

He felt foolish furtively telling his boss that he had to return home at lunchtime, but there was no way around it: he needed to be able to see for himself what was actually happening on the dreaded site. He settled at his computer, and swore to himself when he found that he could not recall his password and would have to set up a fresh profile under a variant of his name and using his corporate email address. He absolutely refused to upload a picture, telling himself that this was because of an unbreakable attachment to his lofty principles, although deep down he knew that it was more because he did not want the world to know what he was up to. After much flailing around, Paul finally found the group that was attacking the product. He was incredulous: thousands of people seemed to have nothing better to do than post insulting comments, links and random messages about his company and its product. Reading this torrent of badly written, ill-informed abuse, he reached an instant decision that he was convinced was the only sensible option in the circumstances. As far as Paul was concerned, these attention-seeking idiots were simply not credible, and therefore they could safely be ignored: and by making that snap decision, and later laying out his recommendation in an elegantly written report, Paul almost got himself fired.

A few days later the story was picked up by the *Wall Street Journal*, which decided that here was a nice illustration of 'citizen activism' up against a leaden-footed company that did nothing to respond to the issues raised, apart from putting out meaningless press releases. Global World Corp, the *WSJ* solemnly informed its readers, was totally out of touch and simply did not understand modern and sophisticated consumers or how to communicate with them in a wired world. Paul had seen a copy of the story and so knew what was coming. Sure enough, he was peremptorily summoned to Pamela's office by a curt email. She told him to shut the door, threw her copy of the *WSJ* down on the desk between them and glared at him:

If we – you – do not turn this around in the next two days, you can start looking for a career alternative.

Although Paul is, of course, a figment of my imagination, I suspect that many readers will have recognised fragments of his life and concerns in themselves, or in others. He is, indeed, a composite, the result of many meetings, discussions and encounters with numerous people who work in all fields of business. I am convinced that many of the Pauls out there are facing a profound existential struggle to understand how they can cope with the changes they are experiencing. To begin to deal with this dilemma, as with most interesting questions, we need to go back to philosophy – and to do that I want to take you back to my time at Oxford, at the end of the last millennium.

PART TWO
Defining a New Language

(4) Shifting Your Perspective

In the summer of 1995, shortly before starting at Oxford, I was told to read *The Problems of Philosophy* (1912), one of many books written by the great English philosopher Bertrand Russell. Its contents came as a shock to me as I was astonished to see that this great man appeared to reduce philosophy to a series of linguistic games and obscure discussions of seemingly pointless topics. One such topic, I clearly remember, was the problem that Russell felt was posed by proving the existence of a table: how, he asked, could we ever know for certain whether a table existed or not? With painstaking logic Russell laid out how difficult it was to prove with absolute certainty the existence of a table – and anything else for that matter. Accustomed as I was to a rather grander vision of philosophy, I was disturbed at the prospect that I would be spending the next three years of my life among people who thought that this sort of inconsequential nonsense was the subject's major problem and one worthy of our close attention.

However, on closer examination I became fascinated by the question, and after a few months I began to see that the 'table problem' was far more fundamental than I had first thought. What Russell had done was to encapsulate two long-standing and competing conceptions of reality: on the one hand, we had an 'objectivist' view of reality – essentially Platonic in nature – which postulated that there is a reality 'outside our minds' and that the goal of philosophers is to try to uncover this reality. This notion is important because it assumes that in all discussions about reality there is a correct answer; thus if we discuss competing views of the world with someone, together, and through the application of logic, we can come to a correct answer. Socrates, who was the main character in Plato's books of course, was renowned as a master at uncovering the truth through his acute questioning; and on the opposite side to the objectivists stood the sceptics. They believed that nothing could be proved with absolute certitude, and thus we were forever trapped in a world of uncertainty.

Although I had studied Greek at school and had a respectful fascination for Plato and his Socratic approach, I gradually started to shift towards a more sceptical position as I had come to feel that it was impossible to prove anything with real certainty. But as soon as I thought I had safely arrived at this new and intellectually impregnable position I sensed that it too was lacking. I did not feel that it was useful in explaining how we actually viewed reality. It was when I read Nietzsche that I found a third way to look at the problem. He did not seem interested in solutions, but he did offer an alternative explanation: there is no absolute and definitive reality, he asserted, only that which can be defined by our multiple and ever-shifting perspectives. Nietzsche called this world of constantly moving viewpoints 'perspectivism', and suggested that we simply needed to accept that the world could be perceived in an infinite number of different ways. At a stroke he had solved the problem of objectivism by stating that it was a futile quest, and had also showed that scepticism without resolution was next to useless, an excuse for doing nothing. It was – and for many still is – an intensely radical proposition, and Nietzsche was lucky that he lived at a time when there was no dominant body that might have taken lethal exception to his ideas. Unlike so many unlucky and blameless souls from earlier times, he could posit his radical notions without suffering the consequences.

THE WITCH'S TALE

Looking at a radical shift in perception, we can see how some key words, backed up by radically new perceptual models, can completely transform how we view certain things.

Let's look at an old lady, living by herself in the countryside but not too far from the local town. She likes to prepare herbal teas, and has knowledge of medicinal plants that she uses to cure her relatives of various ailments. She learned much of this from her own grandmother, and by what we would now call empirical observation. She has no training and no scientific reference texts to rely on, but a lot of what she does appears to work quite well. Her problem is that the year is 1563 and she lives in medieval Europe, in south-west Germany to be precise. The population of sixteenth-century Germany viewed her through the dominant paradigm that combined religious dogma, the unthinking acceptance of authoritative decrees and superstition. She will join a large number of others who ended up burnt at the stake in one of the first – but sadly not the last – major persecutions of alleged witches in European history.

Now let's observe a similar person through a modern paradigm that combines science and tolerance and a restraint on excessive institutional power: she becomes a charming – perhaps slightly eccentric – old lady who shares her wisdom (that we now know has some scientific basis) with her neighbours and friends, all of whom are happy to benefit. It is almost unthinkable that people could ever have reached the brutal and irrational conclusion that condemned this woman's ancient predecessor to an unspeakably terrible death. A shift of paradigm from magic and superstition to science and tolerance has radically altered how we view someone and how we react to them.

Nietzsche's powerful arguments resonated strongly with me: I felt that perspectivism offered an intelligent and practical philosophical standpoint from which to view the world. However, even this theory was not quite enough in itself, and to complete the picture I had to turn to another thinker.

When I came across the notion of 'paradigm shifts', as formulated by Thomas Kuhn in his book *The Structure of Scientific Revolutions* (1962), I gradually made a connection between this theory and Nietzsche's perspectivism. Kuhn was writing about scientific changes that moved in sudden and unexpected shifts because an older paradigm could no longer explain certain phenomena as well as a new paradigm. His insight was to realise that we move from one theory to another in a sudden jolt and not because of wisdom accumulated from the work of previous generations of scientists. Business theorists enthusiastically took up the term and used it to show how companies needed to be able to shift their paradigms in situations where the prevailing orthodoxy could no longer explain what was actually happening in the market place.

For a while the theory of paradigm shifts was compelling, but the inevitable shortcomings quickly became apparent. The theory suggests that once you know which paradigm is the right one, you just need to adopt it and you are fine until the next significant change in the market place occurs; the process of finite and predictable adjustment then begins anew. Two factors, which are especially pronounced in the contemporary world, make this vision unhelpful: radical technological change is happening with increasing frequency, and many of its effects are playing out unseen and therefore hidden from even the keenest onlooker. In fact, the fast-changing world that we now live in has obliterated the notion that we ever can arrive at a settled and predictable destination, and so clearly we now require a more flexible understanding of paradigms. Indeed, I would go further and argue that the new paradigm is that there is no new dominant paradigm, and there might never be one again. In this unprecedented situation I believe that combining the notion of continual paradigm shifts with an understanding of perspectivism can offer us the best approach for coping with an ever-changing reality. In a period of accelerating change, this combination becomes a necessary tool to be able to accept and embrace uncertainty and, more importantly, to understand it.

We all know that certain events which occur – at the personal and historical levels – can come as a complete surprise and with shattering results. Nassim Nicholas Taleb captured the concept of a highly unpredictable event that fundamentally changes the way we see a situation in his book *The Black Swan*.[1] The term 'black swan' itself has a long and varied history dating back to ancient Rome, but by the sixteenth century it was understood to mean a simple impossibility: no black swan had ever been observed and therefore, it was argued with cast-iron logic, one would never be observed. In 1697, however, a Dutch expedition to then unnamed Australia, led by Willem de Vlamingh, discovered the impossible: black swans, and in abundance. The meaning of the expression inevitably changed: something that everyone had thought impossible could turn out to be possible after all. Taleb took the definition and repopularised the concept and the term itself. It is widely used again today, and when one ponders the seismic political events and profound economic turmoil of recent times it is easy to think that we live in an age of increasingly frequent 'black swan' sightings.

What can make a black swan such a dangerous and surprising event is if we hold our personal paradigms to be true and

---

1   Nassim Nicholas Taleb, *The Black Swan: The Impact of the Highly Improbable* (New York: Random House, 2007).

complete; if such is our stance, we dislike it profoundly when inconvenient reality gets in the way. Once we see a black swan it forces us to rethink any number of assumptions, with fear and uncertainty inevitably following close behind. The human mind seems driven to integrate the new black swan, rationalise it and then move on, blissfully unaware that there may be another black swan just around the corner. Many black swans occur as huge events of historic importance, but the most useful are those that occur and result in small and very personal paradigm shifts. Perhaps it is the shift we make when understanding how a particular piece of new technology can work for us, or maybe it is the shift we are forced to concede when we thought we were right about a project and certain it would succeed, only to see it fail for reasons we do not immediately grasp. All learning involves some degree of paradigm shifting, and what we can do at a personal level is willingly embrace large and small paradigm shifts as and when they are helpful. But to do this successfully we need to understand what stands in the way of our shifting paradigms, the barriers that I call the 'paradigm walls'.

The first obstacle we face is the simple fact that paradigms undoubtedly work well as practical tools to help us navigate the ordinary and commonplace events of everyday life. These basic paradigms are hard to give up because they have served us well and often continue to work even after the basis for their usefulness has vanished. With these paradigms we are able to understand complex situations swiftly, and draw conclusions that enable us to make quick and effective decisions. In a business setting, for example, this might mean that because we understand the particular subtleties of the management culture of our company we almost instinctively know how certain things should be interpreted, and act upon them accordingly. Paradigms are the result of experience or learning, and they help us simplify reality so that we do not have to reflect on and ponder every event as if it were the first time we had encountered it. In other words, these paradigms equip us with mental agility and speed of thought. Fundamentally changing perspective often requires a great deal of intellectual effort, and if it is not absolutely essential to make the change then we will often prefer to use the older, tried and tested paradigm.

Although learning to shift paradigm is important, it is by no means easy. The more profoundly this paradigm is intertwined with our personality, the more difficult changing it will became.

THE TERRORIST'S TALE

No paradigm shift is more excruciatingly painful than one that involves abandoning deeply held religious convictions, and no one holds these convictions more profoundly than fundamentalists – Islamic or Christian.

A young man who had grown up as a supporter of terrorism, but had made a recent conversion to fight those he had once seen as his jihadi brothers, told me about the pain he felt when changing his belief system. He described it graphically: think of your brain as a veil of silk that is put on a surface sprinkled with metal spikes. Now imagine you were to suddenly pull away the veil; it would feel as if your brain was being ripped to shreds. This is how, he told me, it felt like to shift his own paradigm. In *The Power of Impossible Thinking* Colin Crook argues that some paradigms – or as he calls them 'mental models' – can have such a profound impact on your brain that they can change your brain's physiology, the way the brain is actually physically mapped.[2]

Thus a paradigm shift is not necessarily just an intellectual concept; it is a physical change in the makeup of your brain. The more embedded

---

2   Yoram Wind and Colin Crook, *The Power of Impossible Thinking: Transform the Business of Your Life and the Life of Your Business* (Upper Saddle River, NJ: Wharton School, 2006).

the paradigm, the more likely it is to be physiologically imprinted in your brain. If this is indeed true, then the pain of changing paradigms becomes understandable. Such existential shifts mean that you redefine your sense of self, your identity and your understanding of reality: a daunting prospect for anyone, but for someone whose beliefs are core to their sense of self it is even more painful.

Most paradigm shifts are, however, thankfully not as traumatic and painful as abandoning one's religious or political faith; but even so, we always seem to have an instinctive resistance to change, and our first reaction is often to try to resolutely defend our existing paradigm before fully exploring the possibilities offered by something new.

As was the case with the reformed terrorist, many people believe that the way they view the world defines who they are. Whatever you call yourself – Christian, communist, capitalist – you tend to perceive this self-definition as an intrinsic part of your identity, joined to some inner core of your being. Any move to change your perception of the world is made difficult by the undoubted strength of this feeling. If we have strong views about something we tend to believe that if our opinion is proved wrong in some way we ourselves are diminished. This makes us more likely to defend opinions and hold on to paradigms simply because we have identified with them so strongly. This is, of course, irrational, and we need to learn to separate our beliefs from our sense of self; it does not make sense to attribute more validity to a belief simply because you feel that it is part of your identity.

Changing paradigms requires mental energy, stamina and, let us not forget, sufficient time to observe the world with the new mindset to see if it actually works and is appropriate. It takes time to make these adjustments, and such a laborious process – which might end in failure if we have chosen the new paradigm unwisely – can mean that we do not necessarily feel that we are getting smarter; on the contrary, sometimes it might feel as if intellectually we are shrinking, maybe even to the point where we feel as though we are starting from scratch. It all adds up to the fact that we have developed an instinctive aversion to the process of change and have created numerous strategies to avoid it.

A final obstacle to shifting a paradigm – one that is perhaps in its own strange way the most formidable – is that embracing a new paradigm can make us look foolish. If you have lived life based on a particular set of beliefs which are suddenly disproved, you are sure to feel discomfited. And then there is the simple fact that most people feel deeply uncomfortable when venturing into new intellectual terrain. This seems particularly true of certain professions where a great deal of emphasis is put on traditional measures of intelligence. Doctors, for instance (upon whom history confers such weighty authority that author Tim Harford used the term 'god complex' especially for them in his book *Adapt: Why Success Always Starts with Failure*), seem able to remember a great number of medical facts but often struggle with computers and new technology.[3] Can it be that with the passing of time there is an increasing resistance to acquiring new skills? It would certainly seem so, and my view is that the high level of competence shown by doctors in one area of intellectual activity makes it less likely that they will feel comfortable in an unfamiliar area where they have to master new skills. The paradigms that we 'own' can make us look good and lead others to regard us as highly competent, but the minute we

---

3   Tim Harford, *Adapt: Why Success Always Starts with Failure* (London: Little, Brown, 2011).

shift to new territory everything changes: we feel vulnerable to exposure and panic can set in.

And yet despite all that I have said, and however hard it may seem, I am certain that being open to endless new paradigms and embracing change will be the key to thriving in the twenty-first century. To become comfortable with ever-shifting paradigms we need to remember Nietzsche and relearn how to constantly adjust our perspective; we need to enter a state of 'permanent learning'. The world is changing at a bewildering pace that shows no sign of slowing. The deeply rooted and stable intellectual mindset that many of us were schooled in may have been appropriate for the predictable but vanishing world of industrial endeavour that produced physical things, but it has not prepared us for what has come in its place.

THE CHILD'S PARADIGM

In today's society there is a myth that some people are creative and some are not, that some people are naturally gifted with technology and some are not. To destroy this myth simply put any child in front of a computer and see what happens: they will instantly appear at ease, and sometimes almost preternaturally gifted. Of course this is merely how things appear to the observer, but undoubtedly children do approach things without preconceptions and they are naturally endowed with a spirit of discovery. It is, consequently, much easier for them to learn without fear and difficulty. Children have a 'soft paradigm' and possess mental models that are not yet 'frozen': when they are presented with something new, they try to learn about it – and do so without resistance. We tend to lose this adventurous spirit as we grow older, and in its place caution takes a firm hold. Adults who have taken this to extremes and have ended up with frozen paradigms find it much more difficult to acquire new skills.

How can we thaw this permafrost of adult caution? Well, one simple way is to rediscover the inner child's sense of wonder and possibility. Go back to a time when you first discovered something new, something that was so incredibly simple and powerful in your eyes that it totally captivated you.

The link to hyperthinking is obvious: hyperthinkers are curious, want to learn and discover new things; they marvel at the wonders all around them. This curiosity can be innate or it can be developed through education, but the inner drive to discover and learn, the ability to ask questions, challenge preconceptions and get genuinely excited about the discovery of something new are all marks of the hyperthinker.

That is why we need new tools and new thinking to understand and cope better in this new world; that is why we need a new word; that is why we need hyperthinking.

⑤ A New Word ... A New Concept

Words are, in my not so humble opinion, our most inexhaustible source of magic.

Albus Dumbledore – Harry Potter
and the Deathly Hallows

Words have a potency that is underestimated – even ignored – by many. Words shape our understanding and our perception of events; words are nuanced and subtle and immensely powerful. That power has been well expressed by the evolutionary biologist Mark Pagel in his TEDTalk video, 'How Language Transformed Humanity':

Each of you possesses the most powerful, dangerous and subversive trait that natural selection has ever devised. It's a piece of neural audio technology for rewiring other people's minds. I'm talking about your language, of course, because it allows you to implant a thought from your mind directly into someone else's mind, and they can attempt to do the same to you, without either of you having to perform surgery. Instead, when you speak, you're actually using a form

of telemetry not so different from the remote control
device for your television. It's just that, whereas that
device relies on pulses of infrared light, your language
relies on pulses, discrete pulses, of sound.[1]

In periods of relentless change, such as the era we happen
to live in, something as simple as a new word can have a
massive impact on those who use it. A new word can assist
our minds to adapt to change, and by consciously shaping its
meaning to help control the process of adaptation it can be a
powerful tool. I must ask the reader's indulgence once again
at this point because I will briefly draw on further personal
experience to illustrate how the particular word that concerns
us here came into being.

After graduating from Oxford with a degree in Philosophy,
Politics and Economics, I continued a project that I had started
while a student. I had launched the first student radio station
in the UK with a full FM licence, and my ambition (which
wasn't entirely realised) was to create a durable institution
that would leave a unique mark on Oxford's landscape. My
interest in communication had started earlier than this: when
I was at school I had launched a student magazine, and I
followed this with a similar project early on in my time at
Oxford, called *House Bound* (the nickname of my college,
Christ Church, was 'the House' so you don't need to delve
too deeply to understand the connection). In my mind, radio
was the next logical step along this particular path of personal
technological evolution, but just as the radio project was
gathering pace I stumbled upon a strange computer network
called the Internet. At the same time as I began to discover

---

1   This was given at a conference I attended in Edinburgh in July 2011. Available at:
http://blog.ted.com/2011/08/03/how-language-transformed-humanity-mark-pagel-on-
ted-com

its immense power I also started to use it very practically and effectively streamlined the organisation of the radio station. It soon dawned on me that this new information channel would change the world. However, at that point my focus was still very much on the radio station and most of my time was occupied with the day-to-day management of the project. After running the station for over two years (and getting the rather archaic distinction of 'young achievers award' bestowed on me by HM the Queen) I decided to start a communications agency. I chose the name ZeitgeistNet (ZN) because I had been attracted to the word *Zeitgeist* and had first used it as the name of the organisation behind the radio station. I was interested in understanding and capturing 'the spirit of the times' as I had decided that the defining features of my business were to be change and adaptation. As I started to build the company I quickly realised that I needed to work with advertising and PR firms to construct my own client base. I noticed that a few individuals that I met in these companies had come to recognise that the Internet was something they would have to deal with, but they were happy to outsource it to people like myself who seemed to pose little threat to their existing business. And so as I made my way in the world of business my first clients were public affairs, advertising and PR companies that needed help in understanding how the Internet was fundamentally transforming what they actually did.

Corporate advertising as it was conceived it the 1980s sometimes had an air of alchemy about it. Through the magic of TV we were told that we could make any product look enticing and sell anything to a gullible audience. I had quickly become familiar with this world, and I remember hearing seasoned professionals in advertising talking about the 'magical power of TV' and how there was little or nothing that big budgets and great artistry could not fix. It was a viewpoint that back then seemed immutable, but it now stands exposed as a broken paradigm. Indeed, it was already obsolete by the late 1990s, by which time it was clear that television was going to change out of all recognition, irrespective of whether people in the industry liked it or not. In fact, many of the executives I spoke to back then seemed in complete denial about what was happening, and even those who saw the inevitability of change were convinced that they had only to draw on their past experience and natural talent to deal with what was coming. I knew that this was not going to be enough, and it was after a particularly frustrating meeting with some television executives in 2000 – a meeting marked by what I saw as hopelessly limited and circular thinking that led nowhere – that I suddenly realised that overcoming this self-evidently broken paradigm needed a new word. Etymological inspiration came to me suddenly and from nowhere: 'hyperthinker'.

As I began writing an email to share my insight with colleagues at ZN I realised that I was, in fact, already hyperthinking. The values that we had developed at the company had already shifted away from the traditions that had been handed down from industrial culture (hierarchy, command-and-control, a limited flow of information and deliberately stifled creativity among the workforce), but I sensed that this revelation would move things to an entirely new level again. The realisation spurred me on and I wrote with barely contained excitement that with this new word and concept we could help our clients start exploring the future and build an entirely new way of doing things. They could become 'professional learners', exploring creative thinking and new technology with the same passionate intensity that they had previously devoted to market research. I felt that my new word described someone special: an individual, a thinker who is constantly busy exercising their thinking 'muscle'; a thinker who thinks about the Web and technology not with fear and despair but with excitement, adrenaline and intense curiosity; a thinker who is always learning. Web searches conducted during that first flush of excitement confirmed – amazingly – that no one else had even thought of the term let alone been using it. It seemed that hyperthinking was the obvious word to describe the 'right' thinking and the right way to think in the age of the Internet.

EDUCATION AND THE VANISHING INDUSTRIAL PARADIGM

I believe that our current education systems are largely based on anachronistic ideas of preparing people to be factory workers or to form part of a managerial and technocratic class that controlled and administered the wealth that industrial societies created. These ideas were appropriate for the time and, by and large, they worked: they turned out armies of people who instinctively understood hierarchies and slotted neatly into the 'command-and-control' structures which dominated the workplace. Indeed, the concept of tight control of the workplace – and the workforce – was very much the dominant paradigm of the industrial age that is, in Europe at least, now passing from view.

So what has taken its place? How do we now produce economic value in a post-industrial world that no longer needs immense numbers of people, marshalled, controlled and deployed in vast workplaces to create tangible products through mechanical and repetitive processes? We have stumbled from that world into this new age, where creative thinking and mental agility are key skills, without any preparation for the uncertainty that we will find. Relying on the comfortingly ordered past of the industrial age will not provide answers to the challenges of the disordered future, or indeed the chaotic present. I believe that to match the wealth-creating achievements of previous generations, intellectually unfettered and creative *individuals*, free from hierarchical control, will play a critical role. And this is happening now whether companies like it or not. Individuals who possess scarce talent and knowledge (literally no one else at the firm may know what they do about a particular project) have already accrued some de facto power in relation to the organisations which employ them. Hyperthinkers consciously go further: their priorities will not be 'how can I fit into the command-and-control structure of the company?', but 'how can I apply my creativity to solve this and any other problem?' And 'how – and when – can I move outside of my remit in order to find a solution?' Given that there is such a deep disconnection between traditional education systems and the world as it now is, it is obvious that educational practice has to be reformed to allow the hyperthinkers of the future to flourish at an early age. I am convinced that today's technology-adept youngsters will be amazed that what I am arguing for will ever have been deemed contentious: to them it will be second nature.

I went to my next meeting with a slide that carried the title 'Hyperthinker' and a few bullet points explaining that this was a methodology that ZN had developed to help ourselves and our clients learn how to adapt our mindset and thinking. I was excited but unsure of how my audience would respond – after all I had just made the word up – but in the event I sensed that they were convinced; better yet, they appeared to believe that it was a real word. Buoyed up by this positive response, I started developing my idea and kept at it for some years, reading widely, talking to people, adjusting and refining the theory in light of what I found. I began to use the word as a 'hook' in various discussions to explain how important our mindset was, and found that as well as relevance in my own professional sphere it had a place in general discussions about education and finding ways out of challenging situations. And as I started to use the word more and more frequently with colleagues and clients it became clear that many people readily identified with the concept. The more I used the word in everyday conversation, the more I realised how important it was to explain precisely what a hyperthinker was and to demonstrate how they could improve their thinking skills in simple and practical ways. My vision became clearer the more I worked to refine the idea: in the midst of apparent chaos people want a freeform *and* structured approach to help them develop a mindset that will make them feel comfortable in the new and technologically charged environment of the twenty-first century. The key to success in this world which we did not ask for – as Darwin would have recognised – will be our ability to adapt to our environment, and I came to see that hyperthinking could facilitate this process. In my presentations to companies, and in innumerable private conversations, I sought to make the term evoke a picture of vigorous and confident people actively striving to acquire new skills to make them successful and adaptable, enjoying life and – a heretical thought this – enjoying the future.

The irony of seeking to achieve what seemed to be the impossible – a new and durable paradigm for an age that has dispensed with fixed paradigms – was not lost on me; the three years I had spent studying broken paradigms from philosophy and economics had not been entirely wasted. But even if it had been possible for me to do so, I did not – and do not – intend to freeze the essence of hyperthinking into another immovable paradigm that will eventually be broken by a black swan. I wanted, and continue to want, the meaning of this new word to evolve as it is used. If I may borrow from economics, the theory of 'reflective equilibrium' – constantly looking from a theory to its practical application and modifying the former – shows how hyperthinking will keep evolving, propelled forward by the constant interchange between its theory and practice. Hyperthinking is not about creating an ideal concept that floats separate from reality. I see it is a practical word that essentially asks 'How do we need to think in this new century? How do we need to approach creativity? How do we need to approach learning?'

I believe that the reason so many people responded to the term is because its two component parts are so powerful: 'hyper' is immediately contemporaneous and evocative of technology, while 'thinking' is perhaps *the* core skill that today's knowledge workers need to exploit to the full. Fused to form this new compound, these two words suggest that you *can* change your thinking for the better, and with potentially limitless results. I felt emboldened during one fine-tuning session when I consulted the *Oxford English Dictionary* and found four different definitions of the word 'hyper'. I immediately saw that these definitions could help us establish the four dimensions that I had already sensed would be the key to hyperthinking. The first definition may be summarised as 'over, above and beyond'; the second is 'linked or arranged non-sequentially'; the third is 'existing in more than three dimensions'; and the fourth is 'emotionally stimulated or overexcited'. We can take each of those four meanings as equivalent to one dimension of the hyperthinker's mindset: the first dimension means thinking about thinking, what is known as 'metathinking'; the second dimension provides us with an obvious connection to the Internet; the third dimension is about the ceaselessly shifting paradigms that pervade our world; and the fourth is about willing and making things happen.

These four basic definitions are not fixed in any sense, but are fluid and aspirational. They are signposts at the start of the journey to becoming a hyperthinker, and if you do decide to undertake that journey you must start directing close attention to these four dimensions. So it will be seen that the word hyperthinking itself is only a trigger, a reminder that you must look at these four dimensions constantly. It is essentially a mind trick to stimulate better thinking. Thus hyperthinking is not just a word: it is an ambition, a way of summarising the important things we should think about when we want to adapt the way we think, especially about technology. And rest assured that there are no formal grades or experts in hyperthinking who can lord it over the rest of us, merely like-minded people who share the same natural curiosity and creative urges. I believe that by using hyperthinking we can all discover (or perhaps rediscover) mutually beneficial and profound values of trust, openness and integrity, and find new skills and talents that we can apply to become more effective as creative people and knowledge workers. Hyperthinking is a way of capturing diverse and seemingly chaotic ideas and notions and putting them together and to good use. It is a word that embodies a concept and a method that can enable people to say quite simply: 'I want to be more effective and here is a system that I can use'. The process of change that most people undergo will not consist of big breakthroughs, but of simple, almost imperceptible adjustments to our habits that cumulatively change the way we think. I am convinced that if your mindset is open and you adopt the right approach and start using the strategies and tools in this book you can actually be an agent that leads the profound changes that are occurring, rather than someone who simply follows them, bewildered and confused by what is happening.

PART THREE

The Four Dimensions of Hyperthinking

hyperthinking *n* a radical philosophical discipline *and* practical thinking process that advocates ongoing intellectual adaptation and development to meet the changes imposed by a rapidly moving, Internet-driven age. Used especially in business and commercial contexts. See also definitions of its four constituent dimensions: **hypershifting**; **hyperlearning**; **hyperlinking**; and **hyperacting**

hyperthinker *n* one who engages in the practice of hyperthinking

hyperthink *vb* (*intr*) **hyperthinks, hyperthinking, hyperthought** to engage in the practice of hyperthinking (either consciously or unconsciously) by adopting the specific set of intellectual tools and thinking techniques set forth in that philosophy

(6) Hypershifting

hypershifting *n* constant and agile mental movement that enables a hyperthinker to improvise and switch with ease between seemingly disparate and even incompatible intellectual positions

hypershift *n* a sudden and sometimes dramatic intellectual shift from one paradigm or mental model to another

hypershift *vb* (*intr*) hypershifts, hypershifting, hypershifted 1 to deliberately imagine and/or create a new mental paradigm as a way of explaining unforeseen changes in a business environment and successfully dealing with the effects of same 2 to examine and specifically challenge fundamental personal values and preconditioned ideas, and thus experience a conscious and controlled change of perception 3 to look at the world from another person's perspective

'When a new and unexpected paradigm emerges we need to hypershift to understand the new reality that this change inevitably creates'.

'I was growing increasingly frustrated with my client until I hypershifted and made a conscious effort to see the world from his point of view'.

Earlier in this book I stressed my belief in the importance of perspectivism in the modern world, and explained how strong and often irrational attachments to our personal paradigms and mental models define the way we see the world and limit our conception of what is possible. Leading on from this I proposed that there are four dimensions to my theory of hyperthinking, the first and most important of which is hypershifting: the ability to change our paradigms and alter our mental models at will. That is the essence of it, but delving a little deeper it will become clear that hypershifting also means having the humility to admit that we do not have the right answers to everything. There is no shame in admitting that we do not know much about much; that is an eternal verity of human existence – as Socrates could confirm if he were around – but learning the skill (and the joy) of hypershifting can help us overcome some of the apparently insoluble problems that this conundrum seems to pose. Teaching ourselves to hypershift at will opens up a world of possibilities from which we can profit.

There are numerous situations in which shifting paradigms may yield rich dividends. The technique can be applied in our personal lives, as we shall see later on, but it is to business that this fundamental tenet of hyperthinking is particularly suited and most necessary. It was always the case that subtle (and supple) thinkers had an advantage in business, but how much more so in today's technologically wired world. I will set out a few examples for us to consider together: all are drawn from life; some are specific and seemingly trivial, while I believe that others illustrate more fundamentally important points about the benefits of hypershifting.

So first of all, a simple one: think of that time you fell out with a colleague, angry because they wanted you to do something you profoundly disagreed with. Your instincts told you that the situation was *this* way; you were sure of it, but your colleague clearly saw it from a different – and, in your opinion, wholly mistaken – point of view. The exchange between you grew tense and deadlock ensued to the detriment of both sides. You walked away from the meeting feeling frustrated and muttering to yourself, 'He just doesn't get it'. Instead of expending all your energy on trying to prove them wrong, either by persisting in your arguments or by making your point in a thousand different ways, try to step back. A way out of the impasse would have been to try to understand your colleague's point of view by deliberately shifting your paradigm to match theirs. Pretending to see the world by wearing their glasses, getting your brain to focus anew and seeing things from their particular perspective will inevitably have produced a few surprises. This doesn't mean that you are in any way agreeing with their point of view, but you are making a profound and genuine effort to understand what they are seeing, feeling and thinking. Instead of resisting their point of view, try to embrace it. Then, after assuming this new perspective, think about how they see your point of view. Try to see yourself entirely from their perspective. Hold that thought until you feel it convincingly. You can now return to the discussion confident of finding a solution. However, if you still feel that they are missing something or that their understanding is flawed, try to reframe the discussion from their perspective. If not, think about shifting your own position. Both of you may have learned something from the introduction of such unexpected thinking to the situation: at the very least you will have defused the tension and remained on good terms with your colleague. Your goal is not to roll over and agree with your colleague, but to reinterpret the situation from a fresh perspective. Once you have explored this alternative view of things you can start looking for new solutions, but most importantly you can emotionally disconnect from your own position – not because you don't feel strongly about what you are saying, but because you understand where your colleague is coming from.

Another easy one: how often have you actually challenged your own definition of your professional self? Whatever your role, I would be willing to bet that at some point when faced with an unfamiliar situation you have said or thought, 'My job is to do X, Y and Z; it's not my job to do anything else'. That is simply not good enough in the world of business today, where needs change at a rapid pace and where most job descriptions simply do not anticipate dramatic change. You must be able to look at any problematical situation that arises, analyse it rationally and think radically about what you can do to solve the problem. I do hear a lot of people say 'I can't do that because it's not in my job description'. The aspiring hyperthinker's response would be to say, 'Well, it might not be my responsibility, but that doesn't matter'. Hyperthinkers want to transform their job, based on the requirements of the situation and the applicability of their skills and talent. They then seek to convince the powers that be that they should be allowed to continue doing this. This constant testing of boundaries is a common characteristic of every hyperthinker I have met; some of them feature in the interviews later in this book. They decide what they should do and they take the initiative to shape their job to do it, even if it means changing and reinventing their job descriptions. The question is: 'If I do something about it, what is going to happen, and will it benefit me?' People feel that if they define themselves in a certain way, or have the definition thrust upon them by a job description, they will find it difficult to move beyond the boundaries that have been created. The hyperthinker fights to get out of this trap, and the way they do this is to hypershift constantly. The job of the hyperthinker is to get things done – regardless of title. At the end of the day they know that they will be judged on what was done, not on how the job description was defined.

But tense business meetings that end with a grudging handshake and tinkering at the edges of a job description are everyday stuff: what about bigger things? What about the serious stuff that goes badly wrong? How is hypershifting relevant then? I have lost count of the number of substantial projects – mainly, but not always, IT related – where all of the participants' inherent energies and talents have been dissipated in endless circular discussions about minute technicalities and reasons why the project might not work. In the most extreme examples these side issues came to assume such importance that they displaced the original goal and became the heart of the project.

THE DOOMED IT PROJECT

A typical example of a project that runs into the sand is that of the company – this one will remain nameless – which overbuilds an IT system.

Someone – no one can now remember who it was – pipes up one day and says 'Let's build a software platform that will run our website, help to organise our communication and create our printed material, and let's start from scratch'. There is a rush of enthusiasm. Inevitably, a large consultancy firm is brought in to do an audit; said firm is handsomely rewarded with hundreds of thousands of pounds for defining what will be needed. No one is surprised when the conclusion is that another few hundred thousand need to be spent to actually build what will be a highly complicated system. Construction of the system gets under way, but soon runs into the sort of morass I have described elsewhere in these pages. Costs escalate and the blame game kicks in; word of the debacle spreads and the project quickly becomes notorious among the staff.

What went wrong here? Why did the company feel that it could trust a consultancy and pay them a colossal sum of money to produce a report, the conclusions of which were almost certainly prewritten? Why were the same old mistakes made? I would argue that the stock decisions of the

---

type taken here make people feel safe by absolving them of the need to make real decisions. And in a strange way this does ensure that everyone benefits: the consultancy walks off with their cut; the IT people stay happily employed and underused and, moreover, their budget grows and as a consequence they get more power within the organisation. In short, vested interests coalesce around a failing project. This cannot be fundamentally sound practice. And yet all the while there was a latent hyperthinker in the team who knew what the system required and could have knocked it together for a fraction of the cost, using open source technology. A ready alternative to the unfolding fiasco was on the company's doorstep, but an inability to take a risk, hypershift and see things from an alternative paradigm was not taken. Result: a mess.

Often it is the case that those involved in these situations end up feeling deeply unhappy because they have lost sight of their original aims; sometimes it can seem as if they never understood in the first place how the project could work and the problem that was being solved by the project. One petulant reaction is that 'if it isn't perfect then it won't work, it can't work and, what's more, it shouldn't work'. Those who claim to want only perfection forget a simple fact: the sooner a project is live and functioning, even in its simplest form, the sooner the benefits start to accrue and feedback from the users can start – and the project can start being genuinely improved. In endlessly waiting to complete the whole process – and to do it to perfection – so much energy can be expended that once it is finished often no one has the strength or the will to then make the most of the results. The lesson is simple: do not to be afraid of failing to reach perfection. Of course certain things have to work, but not everything has to work perfectly. This might seem radical but I am convinced that it is better to have a good idea attempted and imperfectly achieved than a bad idea perfected.

The sort of projects I have described invariably began with a burst of enthusiasm but then stagnated, with familiar results:

project behind schedule; endless and interminable team meetings in which the same old arguments are rehashed; bitter personal clashes; a sense of hopelessness leading to demoralisation of the team involved. The only way out of this quagmire is to take a significant risk and shift paradigms, and I would urge that anyone in this predicament who is seeking a way out should do so without allowing emotion to cloud their judgement. I realise that this is difficult in business, where strong views and vigorous debate are commonplace, indeed necessary, but don't fall into the trap of seeking to shift blame if things do go wrong. The hyperthinker wouldn't do that. Instead, faced with a train wreck of a project they would ask calmly, 'What can we do here together to find a solution – what is the alternative way that we have missed?' This is the reaction of people who can operate in innumerable situations by shifting between paradigms with ease; this is the reaction of the true hyperthinker. They see things in the round and seek to assess all the problems and risks; they endeavour to understand a situation at some level and see the underlying logic, but also the underlying flaws – too much complexity, too many risks, too many obstacles to be able to make something happen. And that is what they set about solving, seeking ideas, critical but constructive comments and practical solutions that can flourish in a new-found atmosphere of mutual trust. And as things evolve, the demoralised, the pessimists and eternal oppositionists we met earlier become convinced – but only gradually because, as I explained earlier, it takes time to adapt to a new paradigm. Eventually these people become advocates, saying that this was a great idea from the beginning. Ultimately, history is rewritten: 'Well, I always thought this was a fantastic idea', says one particular former arch-critic. The hyperthinker will not gloatingly point out the truth of it; he or she will merely sit and smile contentedly at a job well done.

Again and again I have found that teams at ZN that work in the hyperthinking framework of mutual trust, openness and support are more likely to find solutions to problems than those who work in an atmosphere of what is euphemistically termed 'creative confrontation'. We all know that what really happens is that people start opposing each other's paradigms without honestly discussing what it actually is that they are trying to achieve. Hypershifting can help overcome this by creating the necessary atmosphere in which creativity can flourish.

When clients look at a challenge from the same perspective that they have used for decades, they often miss changes that are glaringly obvious. This is not because the changes are hard to see, but because with a traditional mindset the problems are hard to define. Take the story of many Brussels associations, representing the interests of traditional industries across Europe, that suddenly discover intense attacks are mounting against them online. Their first reaction is to dismiss these opponents as highly emotional, unscientific and biased. They struggle to understand why their carefully written white papers (long documents that few people manage to finish reading) and their planned briefings with the relevant 'stakeholders' do not seem to be working. On the one hand they will state that their work has become increasingly difficult in the face of 'unjust' accusations from 'irresponsible NGOs' which do not have the constraints imposed on industries that work within a serious scientific culture and binding legal framework. But the point they are missing is that it is precisely because they have been absent from the online discussion and have not sought to adapt their paradigm to a changing context that things are getting worse. When they – so often reluctantly – agree to explore alternative options, and shift perspectives, they realise that a new language, a new culture and new processes for communication exist. And this new space is not populated by a minority group of enraged and implacable activists, but by people who very much reflect the makeup of 'ordinary' society and who want industry to be a part of the discussion. When the exploration starts, and the experimentation with new communication tools (done with an intelligent strategic perspective) begins, then there is a sense of great excitement and discovery. Twitter, Facebook and Google turn out to be tools that can be used by all sides in the discussion, but the most important shift happens when the mind is open to change and experimentation.

PESTICIDE SHIFT

The pesticides industry is difficult to love and easy to hate. NGO activists find it an easy target for campaigning, and over the years the industry has come to believe that keeping a low profile is probably the best strategy for dealing with the unremittingly hostile headlines. I have some sympathy with this approach: what can you do when the word 'pesticide' itself carries such heavily negative connotations among the general public.

The European Crop Protection Association (ECPA), the organisation that represents the developers and manufacturers of pesticides in Europe, was a ZN client for several years. We had hoped to work on their strategic approach to online communications, but had largely failed to change things in any significant way. Then in 2009 a couple of developments arose that would provide the necessary impetus. The industry was being threatened by European legislation that could significantly impact upon business, and possibly even change the agricultural landscape in Europe. Suddenly the industry realised that despite its detailed research and in-depth network of relations with key European decision makers, the world had started to shift dramatically. It was felt that the legislation didn't make sense and wasn't even based on the numerous scientific studies that had been conducted by the industry.

As the deadline for passing the legislation approached, people grew increasingly concerned. In the past we had already shared some strategic ideas that they had explored but decided not to pursue. Our 'hyperthoughts' involved rethinking the engagement of the industry with the public as well as moving towards a more open, transparent and self-critical style of communication. We had urged them to embrace the Web as a core tool in their attempts to reach out to the public, but largely to no avail. The looming crisis provided just the trigger that was needed to shift things. Friedhelm Schmider, the general director of the organisation, surprised his colleagues by exclaiming: 'Just because I don't understand it, doesn't mean it's a bad idea. Let's just do it! Why not try something else! We need new thinking and this sounds like new thinking!' After giving his broad support for a new approach we got started. As indicated earlier in this book the organisational environment in which you work makes a big difference to how projects can be executed. At ZN one of the reasons we created the concept of hyperthinking was to help us find new clients who connected with the idea so that we could work together on new and innovative projects. Luckily we found just such a person at the ECPA.

Helen Dunnett had been hired by the ECPA as an IT support manager. Her personal journey had been unusual and complex. She has a varied CV that includes artist and photographic stylist to events and public relations manager, to running and fundraising for an NGO. After several career and personal detours she had landed her job as IT manager at the ECPA. When she came across our project she immediately felt that this could be a chance for her to get involved with an exciting project where she could could really make a difference and learn some new things. Helen was – and still is – fascinated by new technology and by the way people use the Web to communicate. She quickly become the main ambassador for this particular project inside the organisation, and was able to sell a new vision for the industry. Slowly but surely she started to shift the debate about pesticides online. This was the first significant step taken by the industry towards greater transparency, one which started a shift in the organisation's culture where it came to see the Web as a core component of its online engagement. The project started with the launch of a simple blog, called pesticideinformation.eu, where the goal was to communicate the issues surrounding pesticides in an open and honest way. We acknowledged that the industry was behind the site, but stressed that it wasn't to be a simple echo of the industry's position. It was there to inform people about the issues and to engage in debate, recognising the concerns people had and the need for real discussion.

As the site started to gain traction with its target audience Helen became the face of the site, interviewing people at events, travelling around to ask farmers, experts, scientists and a range of other people what they thought about the role of pesticides in society. She even managed to interview journalists about what they felt about the issue; turning the tables on them and getting them to assess the complex and interlinked issues of farming, agriculture and pesticides. One of the leading opponents of the industry even took part in a vigorous debate on the site about a legal case she was involved in. The organisation gradually recognised this approach as truly transformative, and as result it adopted a much more open attitude, using new technology as a core strategic tool to engage with interested parties. Helen moved from IT support to e-communication manager, where she continued to pioneer this radical new approach. She was then offered a job at Microsoft, where she helped launch a new online strategy for one of the most recognised companies in the world.

As a true hyperthinker Helen tested new tools and engaged in constant learning. She took a risk and made a real difference to her work – unknowingly redefining her job description by seizing the opportunity to engage in something she was passionate about and then choosing a bold new challenge to take her career forward. I suspect that she won't look back.

But it is not just in business that hypershifting can be applied. The technologies around which so many of these ideas hang pervade all aspects of our lives at home. Take the case of a teacher who told me she does not like technology – full (and emphatically) stop. When she tries to do something complicated with her computer at home there is always – *always* – something that does not quite work the way she wants it to work. So she gives up, or asks somebody else to do it for her because it all seems just too much effort, and … 'I'll never understand it anyway, so what's the point?' Now that is a familiar sounding excuse, is it not? While we were talking, the teacher repeatedly expressed her intense frustration at the situation. That grinding sense of frustration is easily explainable: she thought she should know how to command the computer:

I am an adult, I am intelligent, I am educated, and therefore I should know these things. Not knowing them makes me feel stupid, and therefore I do not want to continue because the more I do it, the worse that feeling gets.

That feeling of inadequacy, of never quite knowing something that always seems just out of reach is a critical negative paradigm; it is a wall that has to be scaled. To think that this person – however friendly and kind – is responsible for the education of my children sends shivers down my spine. What kind of inspiration will she be to children if she cannot understand the most fundamental building block of education: the fact that we need to embrace what we do not know with fascination and curiosity.

For our teacher to shift her paradigm she ought to have said: 'OK, fine, I know I am not very good at this and I do not understand it but that is perfectly acceptable'. She could frame it as a personal challenge, an educational game. The fact she has a natural resistance to the topic makes it all the more interesting, as treating it as a game will teach her not only about technology but also, more importantly, it will teach her about learning. But that is, of course, a huge leap to make for someone who has been used to assuming that not understanding something is bad, and whose undoubted intelligence has fostered a sense of entitlement to instant knowledge. The simple reality is that no one is going to be competent at something if they have not spent enough time on it. Recall what Albert Einstein once said: 'It's not that I'm so smart, it's just that I stay with problems longer'.

So, firstly, accept that new technology can be difficult, or perhaps we should say 'puzzling' – it is a less loaded word; secondly, be prepared to wait and work for an answer: do not expect to find the solution within five minutes. Our teacher here is an interesting, almost textbook example of the 'frozen paradigm' I spoke about earlier: she told me that she had been educated to believe that she was intelligent and so felt that she should always quickly find a solution to any problem. When this desired outcome failed to materialise instantly it not only made her feel stupid, it also made her feel like a failure. And failure is one thing that our society will not tolerate: nothing good ever comes of failure, or so the conventional wisdom goes.

A PERSONAL STORY: FAILURE AND SUCCESS AT OXFORD UNIVERSITY

When I applied to Oxford University I found the whole experience extremely draining. I did not have a particularly impressive academic track record at school and I had studied all my life in Belgium, in a local school where Oxford was not really on the radar. I moved to the UK to prepare for the entrance exam, and noticed that the people I met there had a curious tendency to be impressed by the simple fact that I was merely applying to Oxford. Upon investigating further I found that some bright individuals had chosen *not* to apply to Oxford in case they had to live with the appalling stigma of failure that attached to the 'Oxford reject'. At the time this hadn't really been an issue for me as I thought I was simply applying to a good university, and I was hoping to get in without my life depending on it.

I focused on my preparation and thought I was doing reasonably well given the fact I was adapting to a new education system and was studying in a language in which I had never had any formal education (I was educated in a French-speaking school). So after the year of preparation was over and I had been through the gruelling entrance interviews, I received a letter in the post which turned out to be one of the most memorable I have ever received. It announced that I had not been accepted by the college to which I had applied and that 'despite being a good candidate, he was not good enough to make it into Oxford'. They were not just saying that I had failed because other candidates were better; rather I had failed because I was 'not good enough' for Oxford. The effect of this rejection was devastating: I realised then why so many people chose not to apply, or to keep the fact a secret lest they failed. If they kept the whole thing secret they didn't then have to go back to their friends and relatives to admit they had failed.

When I look at it dispassionately I can see that the interesting aspect about this failure is that it affects your own self-confidence far more than the actual perception that the outside world has of you. It also creates a sense

---

that you are less intelligent then you thought you were, and suggests that you are simply not up to the level of the Oxford student. Of course, the outside world was far less concerned with my situation than I was, but the burden of this failure was heavy and a big blow to my ego.

After much soul-searching and reassurance from a few trusted people that I should ignore the comments in the rejection letter, I decided to try again. This time, however, I realised that to get in I would need to gain a much deeper understanding of how the system worked. Many applicants to Oxford naively believe that it is a meritocratic university which will infallibly select the best and the brightest. As it says in many universities' admission brochures, their advice is to 'be yourself' and you will get in if you deserve to. This is completely misleading and distorts our understanding of the application system. It also relies on a conception that intelligence is innate and that the selection system of Oxford will always pick the best and brightest, hence the exhortation to 'be yourself'. But, like any other institution, Oxford has a set of values, a perception of the outside world and a specific way of evaluating what makes a 'good applicant'. It also holds a view of intelligence that is academic and maintains the aura that its students and alumni are 'naturally' brilliant (the classic image of Oxford was that of students who could display 'effortless superiority' – they could be smart without needing to work hard).

After my traumatic failure I had a choice: I could either believe that I was simply 'not smart enough' to get in or I could challenge that paradigm and believe that getting in was a matter of understanding the 'invisible rules of the game' and learning to play by them. I gradually came to understand that the most important factor in being able to get into Oxford is whether or not you understand 'the system' and what the interviewing tutors are trying to find out. Having decided that I would give it a second try, I undertook to understand the tutors' selection criteria. I had to translate some of my thinking into the Anglo-Saxon frame of mind. By the time of my second round of interviews I perceived this process much more like a game in which you had to understand the rules, rather than a test of raw intelligence.

I was successful the second time round, but my feeling was very different from that of many of my peers. I didn't feel that this was a vindication of some natural intelligence or genius that I possessed. I just felt that I had understood the system better than others and had worked 'smart' on the skills that were needed to get through. But the lessons from this failure were deep and powerful. They taught me the importance of not allowing others to define you by their standards, and not to accept being branded a failure. Failing is the most important stage of learning and, as every entrepreneur worth their salt will confirm, failure is the engine of growth and development. I also learned that society's conception of 'natural intelligence' could have a devastating effect on you – if you let yourself believe it. You need to be able not just to shift your paradigm but also to choose your paradigm.

A way out for our teacher would have been for her to cheerfully accept that she is not an expert with the technology that so baffled her; and nor should she be looking – or expect – to come up with a specific solution in a short period of time. And it turns out that another teacher in my son's school actually did something along these lines that proves the point exactly. Happy to admit that she was not a technophile, she asked the children to make a presentation to her about iPods, smart phones, PlayStation's, Xbox's and all the other devices that she kept hearing so much about but of which she understood very little. As a result the children spent several weeks preparing the presentation (using a laptop and a beamer and bringing along all their favourite gadgets). This was one of the best projects they did, and their starting point was their teacher's ignorance. The process turned them into teachers, and the fact that they knew that the teacher was genuinely interested in learning about something she didn't understand increased their motivation and made them fully engaged with the project. Unlike the first teacher I talk about, this one acted like a true hyperthinker and turned her ignorance into a massive learning opportunity not just for her but also for her class. If you face a similar dilemma to our first teacher then accept that it might take longer than you would like to find an answer, and realise that that is fine. In fact, say to yourself that the only way I am going to learn is not by working at this but by *playing* with it. The substitution of play for work is liberating and can only be a good thing: it is fun, it is what children do. They do not actually go around saying they know how to do anything, but they play with something and if it takes five minutes or five hours it does not matter: they get there in the end. If you want to learn how to use technology you have to cultivate a similar mindset to a child and try different things constantly. If and when it doesn't work it is not failure: it is simply playing, and occasionally you will make a breakthrough. It will give you some satisfaction, but never forget that this is now a constant process – the game, and a game is what it is, never stops.

But developing the art of shifting paradigms – business or personal – is a difficult one to master and it takes practice, lots of it. The good news is that the mental exercises which will lead to an increased ability to shift paradigms can be done anywhere. Choose a topic when you are on the way to work; make it one about which you have strong – perhaps immovable – feelings. Now force yourself to adopt a different stance; immerse yourself in a new paradigm and see how the world looks. If you need some help with this buy a newspaper whose political stance you disagree with. You will know full well the rubbish you are going to get from the resident pundit who has an opinion on everything and who never suffers from self-doubt about anything, but read what they have to say anyway. Engage with their arguments; assess them coolly and dispassionately, and admit – honestly now – if they have any merit. Force yourself to adopt these views and, again, see how the world looks different. None of this need be a permanent shift – that is the whole point – and you can return to familiar and comforting terrain as soon as you like. It may not have done much for your blood pressure, but the point is that you are gaining practice at shifting paradigms. The next time you are in a heated meeting at work actually listen to what your 'opponents' are saying; master your emotions and admit frankly if there is substance to what they are suggesting; more importantly, seek to empathise with the other viewpoint so that you can truly engage with it. You may even wrong-foot them by conceding as much. Another useful exercise is to write down five dominant preconceptions you feel about a particular subject; then describe five alternative views of the same subject; and then, if you find that you are really on a roll, write down five more. Pretty soon you'll have pages of ideas and will have explored the subject in full. I am sure that you will find it intellectually exhilarating to stretch your mind in this fashion.

The type of nimble intellectual footwork I have just described is far from the norm. How many people do you know who deliberately buy a newspaper (or look at one online) whose political views differ from their own? Most of us seek reinforcement of what we already believe, but if you continue with these simple exercises you will become adept at making abrupt mental shifts. You will see and understand situations from a variety of perspectives and will be able to articulate views that may take people by surprise. Colleagues and clients will see that you look intelligently at problems from a multitude of angles and then, and only then, reach a decision; they will come to trust, perhaps even envy, your judgement. You will be able to start defining yourself by your understanding of multiple perspectives and not by being attached to one single worldview. Learning that perspectives can appear inherently wrong when viewed from another perspective is a key insight into hyperthinking. Once you understand that there is no 'true' perspective you can become more comfortable in shifting, and you can learn to separate your ego from your perspective.

I hope that I have convinced you that hypershifting has instant application everywhere in the real world and can be applied in myriad different situations, in general discussions and to specific problems. If nothing else, remember that it is fun: you can play around with the concept of altering your viewpoints at any time and with anyone. The key practical points are as follows:

- Strive to be more aware of your preconceptions and unconscious assumptions in any given situation – in other words, the elements that form your current mental model.

- Do the same for the people you are working with: think yourself into *their* paradigms and identify *their* preconceptions and unconscious assumptions.

- Challenge your assumptions about your work, your industry or a given project you are working on. Form an alternative perspective and explore this perspective to see if it brings you new insights.

- Connect apparently unrelated subjects or disciplines to see what insights you can create: look at a political problem through a scientific framework, an artistic one through a business one and vice versa. The more unexplored connections you make the more new insights you will create that might offer you new solutions to problems.

- Challenge yourself intellectually to change your preconceptions – *even if you don't need to*: the practice will be good.

- Don't give up just because something seems hard and progress is slow.

- Don't be afraid of failure: it's not the end of the world – in fact it is the beginning of learning.

- Don't bluff, and be confident in telling people that ignorance is nothing to fear.

- Don't be afraid to play, but remove negative emotions from the game and take your ego out of your paradigm.

- Be solutions obsessed: be relentless in your pursuit of solving seemingly unsolvable problems, and make a point of spending more time with the problem.

- Write stuff down: a diary of paradigm shifts would make for interesting reading and it would also be educational, which brings me to …

⑦ Hyperlearning

hyperlearning *n* the practice of constantly seeking out new and unfamiliar topics, and intellectually exploring them in novel and vigorous ways (NB said to be most effective when it takes place outside traditional academic or structured learning environments)

'Creativity is a learned skill, but like any skill it requires regular practice to develop it fully. Daily hyperlearning at every opportunity is a must for the modern and forward-thinking executive'.

hyperlearn *vb* (mostly *intr*) hyperlearns, hyperlearning, hyperlearned or hyperlearnt 1 to continually gain knowledge and/or practical skills, more especially by adopting and applying the specific tenets of hyperthinking 2 to enhance individual and team creativity through the deliberate use of certain well-defined intellectual tools and techniques 3 to apply constant practice and time investment to ongoing learning

'In today's fast changing world, business executives need to hyperlearn and make the acquisition of new knowledge, insights and skills part of their ongoing routine. If we are to stay relevant to the challenges that tomorrow will bring we need to start and end the day by educating ourselves'.

You will have gathered that one of the key assumptions of the hyperthinking theory is that our education systems are deeply inadequate to meet the needs of the information age. My view is that the two biggest holes in education are the absence of learning to think about thinking, and the persistent disconnection between learning and 'real life'. For modern 'knowledge workers' learning has become more critical than it has ever been before, but what we learn and how we learn has not fundamentally changed from the days when schools turned out young people to fit the rigid structures of industrial society. This cannot continue. Our educational systems need to change, and although some in the field have recognised this and are at last starting to debate the way forward, as traditional 'thinkers' not doers educationalists are likely to be talking about the problem and not actually solving it for a long time to come.

Perhaps worse than realising the flaws in our education systems was the depressing revelation that the bureaucrats at the heart of the educational establishment – the very people who claim to be the official advocates of learning – are slow to accept the need for society as a whole to move to a 'learning-centric' culture. Indeed, when you consider their resistance to the educational potential of new technology, the lack of imagination in the people who actually run schools, colleges and universities is astonishing. The attitude of many of them seems to be that once people emerge blinking into the light from the formal education system that is that – their job is done. The essential fact that they fail to grasp is that learning takes many forms, and can – indeed, must – continue throughout one's life: it should be as natural as breathing that we continue to learn, so the job of a formal education should be to prepare one for permanent, self-made education for the duration of the student's life. As it is, the bureaucratic conservatism that underpins the whole system rubs off on the people who go through it; somehow school and university seem to leave us poorly prepared to continue *self*-educating, and when the formal schooling system is done with us the inherent learning urge seems to dry up in many people. Perhaps it is because traditional – and for many people damning – notions of what constitutes intelligence stalk and follow us all our lives, defining some of the choices people make and undermining their confidence in their own creative abilities. Not only is failing to realise their own potential creativity tragic for them personally, it also has seriously negative implications for our society as a whole. We cannot afford to waste any more of our talents.

All of that is the subject for another book, however. The majority of people reading *this* book will have long since passed through school and university, and as individuals living in the here and now there is no point waiting an age for someone to design an education system from which we will not benefit. We need our learning to start changing now; we need our learning habits to shift. Hyperthinking answers these needs. One of the pillars of hyperthinking stems from the 'above and beyond' element that forms the second dimension, what I have termed 'hyperlearning'. The concept is quite simple: hyperlearning means thinking about thinking and learning to think better and to develop your creative muscle. The assumption is that thinking and intelligence are mainly acquired skills, and that with the right attitude and with hard work and practice you can expand your thinking abilities considerably. Thinking is a muscle that can, based on the amount of mental exercise we are willing to do, be developed and strengthened. We need to treat this 'mental exercise routine' as important as our physical well-being.

But this is not just about completing crosswords and playing sudoku to keep our minds alert, helpful and stimulating though those activities are; it is about stretching our minds further to keep them agile and responsive. We need to challenge the notion that some people are born creative and others are not. Creativity is one of the thinking muscles that we need to develop throughout our lives. Although children start their intellectual lives with a large dose of innate creativity, our educational environment gradually punishes the trait, and this skill seems to be progressively removed from most children. We need to understand that creativity can be learned and taught; and, as with any other form of physical activity, the right exercises with the right tools produce hugely beneficial results. We can learn to think more creatively and improve every aspect of our thinking by learning a variety of techniques and then practising them constantly. In the hyperthinking system we seek to develop a personalised thinking toolkit. This means spending time finding tools that are interesting, exploring them and then using them on a regular basis. I must stress that I do not believe that there is a single set of tools that works for everyone: hyperthinking is not so crudely prescriptive a system. You need to find the right mental exercises that suit you, and then explore and exploit them. These tools can be very simple ones which help you brainstorm or look at a problem from a different perspective; they could even include mechanistic ones to keep your memory fit – learning by rote does have *some* uses. Indeed, some of the techniques I list below are well known and I acknowledge my debt to previous thinkers in the field. What I wish to stress here is the absolutely vital importance of ongoing effort and discipline to continue searching for new tools and techniques and then testing them to breaking point. Inevitably you will become proficient at the ones that seem to give you the best results, but when that happens make sure you do not become complacent; strike out and find new territories to explore.

To give you an example of the kind of tools that I use personally and that have been popular with some of my colleagues and clients I recommend trying some of the following.

- Lateral thinking and thinking-hats: Edward de Bono, one of the first people to highlight the importance of learning to think creatively, invented the concept of lateral thinking, which is the basis for a series of thinking techniques that can help us learn creative thinking. His book on lateral thinking gives a solid framework for the concept, and I particularly enjoyed his book entitled *I Am Right, You Are Wrong*, which he wrote to explain the limits of our rational left-brain thinking model – which needless to say dominates our academic establishments. One of the most practical and straightforward tools he developed in another book is called *Six Thinking Hats*. These techniques are a great aid to hypershifting as it gives you a system to see the world through different perspectives.[1]

- Mind mapping: This was invented by educational consultant Tony Buzan as a way to visualise information in a more effective way. His concept started with the notion that in order to remember information we need to change the way we take notes. Mind mapping has now become a widely practised technique for note taking, project management and brainstorming, and a series of software programs that are available will enable you to

---

1   Edward de Bono, *I Am Right, You Are Wrong: From This to the New Renaissance, From Rock Logic to Water Logic* (London: Viking, 1990); *Six Thinking Hats* (Boston, MA: Little, Brown, 1985).

develop mind-maps on computers, smartphones and tablet devices.

- Apply Kaizen thinking: This is my personal interpretation of the Toyota Kaizen theory of production, as it might be applied to thinking. My assumption is that just as the Kaizen theory of constant improvement can be applied to industrial production, so it can also be applied to the thinking process. By consciously observing *how* we think when we tackle a problem or a challenge we can find small ways in which we can improve our thinking (for example by stepping back, shifting perspective and looking for new ideas). By applying incremental changes to our thinking processes we can drive dramatic improvements in the long run.

MORE ON KAIZEN THEORY

At Toyota they apply Kaizen theory, in which small and incremental improvements are made on a continuous basis, eventually changing things in a dramatic way. One example – at first sight so insignificant as to be absurd – is where the company moved photocopiers in certain rooms in order to cut down the time it took for workers to use them. By proving that it was possible to save 7 seconds in one room, Toyota ended up saving thousands of hours when the change was then replicated everywhere else. The moral of the story is obvious: small changes can make a massive difference.

They may not consciously apply the theory, but Apple also embodies it. For the latest release of OS X they upgraded their software for the iPad, the iPhone and the Mac and in this process they actually improved hundreds of things on all their products in the operating system. They have done so despite being the market leader with a huge competitive advantage and a loyal customer base. Despite all that, Apple still had the passion and motivation to say 'How can we take this even further?' Provided it maintains that sort of commitment it is hard to see how the company cannot fail to dominate the market for decades to come.

- Challenging thinking: Try doing mental arithmetic and refuse to use the desk calculator. Don't forget to keep your brain active in traditional disciplines, and find opportunities to play in order to keep your thinking muscle in shape. Luminosity.com has a series of 'brain games' that can be played on the Internet or on a mobile phone, and which can help keep your memory and critical thinking sharp.

- Brainstorming: alone and in groups. Creatively spark off each other. Quantity not quality is key here.

- Brain-dumping: a useful clearout if something isn't working. It gets you back to first principles. Use a mind map to dump all the information you have in your mind about a give problem; pull together the information in branches. Once everything can be seen in front of you, go for a walk. Then come back and revisit the map and find at least three possible solutions to your problem.

- Problem solving: Take a physical object to pieces and see if you can work out how to put it back together again. Do it alone or in teams.

- Puzzles and quizzes: simple, but effective and not to be underestimated.

When faced with a difficult situation in business or in life that requires careful thought, be sure to decide which hyperlearning tool is the most suitable application. Stepping back in a situation and identifying it as one that requires 'hyperthinking' is the first step. The second is to consider what tools and techniques can help. I often find that mind-mapping is a good place to start as it enables you to capture the different thoughts, ideas, facts and issues that surround the situation. The third step is to look at how you want to tackle things, and which tools will help you to generate the necessary new perspectives and ideas. This is where the de Bono style thinking hats come in handy, especially when combined with more traditional brainstorming techniques to generate new ideas. I will return to these techniques in Chapter 10 where I will explore in more detail how you can apply these tools to your everyday life. What is important is to make time for this process and deliberately seek out new ideas and new perspectives. By connecting apparently disconnected ideas you will find novel insights and new ways of tackling the challenges that you face. It is also an opportunity for putting these new tools to the test to find out which ones generate results for you personally.

You will find that some tools are much more suited to a certain kind of thinking and these will help you get results much faster. If the situation is very challenging, and you find yourself stuck, take it as an opportunity to test a series of tools and see whether a solution can be found. That way you can look at this area of hyperthinking activity as useful on two levels: first, it might actually help you to find a solution to your problem; and second, it is part of your training process and will improve your mind's ability to work by exercising your thinking muscle. By approaching things this way every new challenge can be seen through the hyperlearning prism, while at the same time being an integral part of your personal development. You can also pick problems or challenges that are absurd or have little relevance to you directly, just to exercise your thinking muscle. This might also generate some surprising insights.

Finally, applying yourself with focus and dedication to a problem that you know for a fact has no apparent solution can also be a great way to exercise mentally. By doing this, you free your mind from the stress caused by 'needing to find a solution' and you can think creatively of what might happen if you look at things from a different angle. A solution might just be found when you least expect it, but if it doesn't you will have improved your patience and perseverance – something, as I mentioned earlier, that was what made Einstein look smart. Once you get into the habit of using these tools you will come to enjoy it and – perhaps more importantly – benefit from it. But all of this would be worthless unless we then decide to act upon what we have learned; I'm saving that for the last dimension.

$\textcircled{8}$ **Hyperlinking**

hyperlink *vb* (mostly *intr*) **hyperlinks**, **hyperlinking**, **hyperlinked 1** to explore and study new and emerging Internet technology through direct experience, experimentation and playful interaction **2** to wire and connect an endeavour (especially a business undertaking) with technological tools, thereby enhancing its impact

'By hyperlinking our video with friends and family through social media channels the growth of this campaign was exponential, and we rapidly hit the mainstream media'.

The third dimension of hyperthinking is hyperlinking. Although the impact of new technology underpins the whole of this book, it is this third dimension that connects most directly to the importance of the Web, which as we all know has produced a radical reconfiguration of society in an incredibly short space of time. The Internet, and all of its associated digital information networks, has changed – and continues to change – what we see and the way we see it, the way we process information, the way we communicate and the way we network. We need to acknowledge that this immense shift in the structure of our society has taken place, and look at it without fear. In a practical sense, hyperlinking in our everyday life is simple: it is basically about embracing new technology to the full, and I make no apologies for the evangelical tone that the reader will find in this chapter: Facebook, LinkedIn, blogging, tweeting … this stuff will, if handled properly, make your life better – and I urge you to get involved.

The world of Internet networks offers us extraordinary opportunities for connecting with like-minded people, for learning and for sharing; but, as we shall see, even so-called 'Web-natives' do not make the most of the technological gifts which we are fortunate enough to have been offered. Indeed, I have noticed how strange it is that people who work with computers on a daily basis seldom maximise their potential; these people can even seem to appear curiously uncomfortable with computers. This is where hyperthinking can help: we hyperthinkers need to be positive, proactive and fully engaged with the Web: it is, after all, the perfect medium to satisfy our insatiable curiosity, restless thinking and desire to learn new things and convert our ideas into action. But before talking about that further, I want to address head on some of the fears and criticisms that continue to dog the Web and new technology in general. We are now over 15 years or so on from the Web's arrival in most people's lives, and yet still the prophets of doom refuse to go away. If you harbour any negative feelings about the Web I hope that by the end of this chapter they will have been dispelled. Remember, no one owns the Web: it is ours – we can do with it as we please.

The first thing to deal with is the myth of information overload. Many people express terrible anxiety at the number of emails, text messages and other information delivered electronically. They are especially exercised by the additional workload that this torrent of information supposedly creates. I think that this is a figment of overactive imaginations. Why, when you go into a library, do you not feel overwhelmed by the information overload that you experience visually? There are thousands of books stacked all around, and yet no one feels overwhelmed and depressed by the spectacle. The reason is self-evident: you do not have to read *all* the books. You instinctively exercise restraint and discrimination, and you walk through a library looking for particular books that you want – or merely browse (sound familiar?) in your own time. The analogy with the Web is exact: you choose to go online and look for what you want. It may be a new environment for the storage and usage of information, but it is not something that controls you; you can switch off your computer at any time. If you need to concentrate on something important then close off a certain amount of time and focus on that task. Yes, you may have 200 emails in the in-box, but you do not have to read them all at the same time, and we all know full well that a good proportion of them will contain absolutely nothing of value anyway.

- Prioritise: open these emails and briefly check what is actionable or not actionable. The minute you spot something of genuine value or importance immediately decide how to deal with the information.

- Remain in control: if you overcomplicate things and needlessly overprocess information, of course you will get confused.

So please stop believing the myth of information overload. There is nothing on the Internet that unleashes a torrent of information that will sweep you away the second you log on. Even in a busy workplace where information is pinging around at great speed you still retain the ability to discern between what you need and what you don't need. The traditional skills and virtues that enable us to make the most of books in a library apply equally to the Internet:

- Learn how to find your way around the sections that you find most helpful.

- Remember sites that had particularly easy layouts, and revisit them.

- Take a note of things that you like.

Remain focused and there is nothing on the Internet that will overwhelm you; it is merely our perception – itself created and fed by doom-mongers – that makes it appear so.

Needless to say it is not just the amount of information that the critics complain about; they have other, more fundamental worries. In his recent book *The Shallows: What the Internet is Doing to Our Brains*, Nicholas Carr does make a very interesting point when he says that our brains are being transformed by the Web – and not, he argues, for the better.[1] He maintains that we are now unable to concentrate; we keep jumping from one piece of information to another without absorbing any of it, and this is changing our ability to read in depth and to focus. It is also changing our creativity and our ability to make genuine links between different ideas and concepts. Carr is nostalgic for the vanishing age of printed books, and his tone is largely negative, which is curious because he clearly has

---

1   Nicholas Carr, *The Shallows: What the Internet is Doing to Our Brains* (New York: Norton, 2010).

some interest in the potential benefits of technology. He goes on to point out that parallel to this complete shift in the way we think and seek information has been the emergence of social networks that are completely transforming the nature of the relationships we have with each other. I would agree with that, but where Carr and I disagree is in how we face these facts. I am convinced that we can direct these processes and make them work to our advantage, whereas Carr's is a pessimistic and bleak message that essentially says humanity is starting to unravel as it becomes unable to relate to itself in any meaningful way. Let's leave aside the debatable assumption that humanity was ever ravelled in the first place, and look at the current reality.

I'll start with teenagers, as it is they who are said to be leading us on the march back to the caves. Yet the teenagers growing up today and using Facebook to communicate with their friends are no different from our grandparents using the telephone to arrange dinner with someone at a restaurant. Teens see Facebook as unthreatening and totally natural: they have mastered its basics, they like it and therefore they do not question it. The adults who do not like Facebook, on the other hand, rail against it and deplore it, claiming that 'virtual friendships' are nothing of the sort: what passes for friendship on Facebook is a debased corruption of the true meaning of the word. Well maybe, but my answer to them – and the author of *The Shallows* – is that this is the way things are going to be, and there is not much we can do to stop it. Change is here, the transformation is occurring (arguably, for these teenagers it has already occurred) and we who knew the world as it was before these networks arrived need to stop moaning and think about the best ways we can adapt to our changed circumstances. There is undoubtedly a vacuum here, and by consciously moving into this intellectual space the hyperthinker will have the opportunity to observe technological change at close quarters, find the best way to engage with it and forge a path for others to follow. Indeed, I would argue that if – and I think that it is a big if – things are as bad as others say, then we could help teenagers by showing them that they don't know half as much about technology as they think they do. There is much more to be discovered.

WEB-NATIVES, OR ARE THEY?

When you meet so-called 'Web-natives' (15–17-year-olds who are immersed in technology and cannot imagine a world without it) the easy assumption to make is that they work naturally with computers and certainly don't need our help. Do not be fooled: just because a young person has a Facebook profile and can download files from the Web, it does not mean that they actually know how to correctly and usefully engage with the technology, be proactive about it and build something of genuine and lasting value.

If you want proof of this, watch the YouTube video 'An anthropological introduction to YouTube' by Michael Wesch, an Assistant Professor of Cultural Anthropology at Kansas State University and author of the brilliant video on YouTube called 'The Machine is Us/ing Us'. This online lecture lasts over 55 minutes and has been viewed almost 2 million times. Professor Wesch teaches an anthropology class and he asks his students to experience the Web as if it were an anthropological environment. You will see that he is surprised at how little real, thoughtful experience the students actually have on the Web. He explains that the class is going to create a video and upload it to YouTube; and it transpires that a lot of the students – possessors of smartphones, tablets and all the rest of the must-have paraphernalia – have never actually done this.

YouTube is essentially about a small group of people creating videos for a large group of people, and although YouTube is very democratic, and anyone *can* do it, it does not mean that everyone *does* do it. Making your first video on YouTube is quite a strange experience, especially when you are having what Professor Wesch calls 'a-synchronous conversations'. You upload a video in which you talk to an audience, but you do not know who you are talking to, whether they will listen and if they will reply. You are really talking to yourself, but you think this conversation might reach the entire universe.

> It is clearly a very strange feeling, and Wesch insists that all of his students go through the process. Watching them stumble through the experience is fascinating. How right the professor is to say, 'Do not take for granted that the students know how to do all this stuff, they might never have done it'.

However, there is no denying that to get to grips with the wired world the aspiring hyperthinker will need to make a sustained effort: it will mean attempting to understand how the world of electronic information is organised and how it may evolve (although none of us can know the answer to that, it is fun guessing). And alongside honing our conceptual understanding we must acquire and improve our practical skills. There is no reason to be intimidated by this: it is, at bottom, akin to learning the rudiments of a skill such as carpentry. For example, there is software out there which allows you to see and modify some of the code behind a website. It is called Hackasaurus,[2] and it is a nice way to deepen your connection with technology. Find this software, activate it and take a look at a web page; put on your 'goggles' and see the codes behind the images; see how you can move those images around – be active and playful.

Mark Surman of the Mozilla Foundation is quite right when he says that you should not just be a passive recipient of information from the Web: you should be an active agent, comfortable with the fact that you have the power to transform the online environment. We have already seen the emergence of this transformative element with social media – uploading videos on YouTube, tweeting and so on – and it is clear that people like it. But it is so much more than the mere frippery that opponents always complain of. Provided you make the effort to learn and educate yourself you can

---

2 See http://hackasaurus.org

actually be in full control of these technologies, the very opposite of the situation propounded by the Nicholas Carrs of this world. And if you are looking at its relevance to business then the possibilities really start to become serious: think back to Aurélie's story at the start of this book for proof of that.

If messing about with the structure of websites seems a tad too complicated and does not appeal, then there is one very easy way to start actively engaging with the wired world. Say that you have an interest in a particular author: they normally have a web page or a blog, so why not write to them? The first time I wrote a comment on bestselling author Tom Peters' blog and started to have a conversation with him was an exciting moment. I was taken aback to realise that it was actually him responding. On several other occasions I have put questions directly to authors through their blogs, and when I get an instantaneous response it reinforces my belief that we are now all incredibly close to everyone else. Despite what our opponents say, online relationships are valuable and meaningful – and they are open to all of us. You too can enter this vast and extraordinary community: whether through blogs, Wikipedia or other online portals you can approach people, work in groups, pose problems and try to collectively find solutions; suggest ideas to others and redefine certain things – let the world know what's on your mind. In its magnificent entirety Wikipedia is a great example of what can be achieved by collective effort, but it also offers the chance to put into practice what I have been talking about: do not just read an article there – explore what is behind the scenes and discover how the article was selected or, indeed, rejected. Modify an article yourself, or create a new one, and then sit back and see what happens. Joining the conversation will be fun *and* educational (in the truest sense of that word).

But I see that my excitement has run away with me again. As we saw with the teacher we met in Chapter 6, this sort of creative engagement with technology can be difficult for many people, and for some the easy temptation will always be to walk away and hand the job over to someone who is 'qualified' to do it. So I say again that we must overcome this childish (as opposed to childlike) technophobia and understand that we are all qualified: the hyperthinker wants to initiate things and lead change, and that means opening the Web's bonnet and seeing what the engine looks like. The image is wholly appropriate: peeking behind a website at the hidden wiring is no more of a challenge than taking a look at a car engine was for our great-grandparents. And, just as with a car, what you will find behind a website is not a mystery that only the new priesthood of technocrats may decipher, but a logical construction that can be understood, disassembled, altered and improved to how you want it. So for the adventurous among you, take an iPhone and 'jailbreak' it (which simply means installing software that breaks the Apple environment) and you can suddenly install a variety of new software on it as you are no longer in Apple's 'walled garden'. This can become very messy, but it is how real creativity takes place online. And if you have second thoughts you can go to your factory settings and return to the safe walled gardens of the Apple Universe. Simply by asking the question, 'If that can be done here, maybe it could be done there' you have started 'hacking' your world, and I have no doubt that in exploring these new horizons you will find some very surprising answers.

So far I think that what we actually have is a situation where the positives far outweigh the negatives. Not much controversial about that. Where I may depart from the technophile consensus, however, is when I say that we are nowhere near utilising these technologies to their full potential – and I am not just talking about the 40- and 50-somethings who might feel as if they are desperately playing catch-up. Consider the much-maligned teens we mentioned earlier. I have stressed before how they get comfortable with technology by playfully immersing themselves in it, but that does not necessarily mean that they are learning to think in the right way about what they have at their fingertips – or indeed to think in a particularly creative way at all. In fact, as I have explained, our school and university systems actually teach them not to think creatively. Predictably, the result is an inexorable narrowing of their vision – they reach a comfort zone with technology and then remain stuck there, doing little more than posting pictures of drunken nights out and facile messages that only their friends will understand. Now of course that is something that we *could* be critical of, but it is important to retain a sense of perspective – we are talking about teenagers here after all.

It is my hope that in the long run young children will escape the deadening hand of traditional education *and* the innate conservatism of the teenage culture that awaits them. I hope that they preserve their first and best instincts and continue to explore, happily making mistakes and failing and learning to be inveterate tinkers. But I fear that in the short term at least, that may be wishful thinking. As things stand, I sense that we hyperthinkers have a serious job on our hands saving many teenagers from atrophying. We need to demonstrate that their initial urge to push at the limits of technology and find out more must never be allowed to wither and die. We come back to the fact that it is all about one's mindset and attitude: if you are open and curious, playful and inclined to explore, and happy to make mistakes then you will benefit from applying hyperthinking to the Web.

Even technological evangelicals like me must occasionally pause to exercise caution, and so here is something to bear in mind. The Web is a work in progress and may remain so for ever; we will never arrive at a 'finished' Web, although that will not trouble the hyperthinker who has dispensed with limiting paradigms. In fact, we are still at an early stage in the Web's history, and no one can be sure of where we are going. The virtual world is still being created piecemeal; bits of it are being fine-tuned to near-perfection, while other bits are being discarded. Such is the pace that even the people at the heart of the drama do not know precisely what is going on. The programmers who created Twitter did not actually know what people were going to do with it. They had no idea it would grow so fast and they had no idea it would be used in the way that it is. Do not be downhearted by the fact that no one knows what is going on: revel in it. Remember that it is the programmers who are struggling to keep up with the creative users, as they are the ones who are driving change – an astonishing inversion of the normal creator–consumer relationship that was once thought to underpin technology and created so much unnecessary unease in people.

(9) Hyperacting

hyperact *vb* (*intr*) **hyperacts**, **hyperacting**, **hyperacted 1** to turn an abstract idea or concept (especially in business) into a reality through focused, concerted and determined action that is the outcome of hypershifting, hyperlearning and hyperlinking **2** to adapt and change an existing project and its underlying assumptions when faced with an unforeseen change in circumstances by the use of imaginative and sustained effort and action

'We thought that our plan was great and that we had a clear grasp of the market. How wrong we were! When we started rolling out the product we realized that we had completely misunderstood local sensitivities. Our roll out was already deployed, but by hyperacting quickly and effectively we were able to reposition the product to serve a different – and more appropriate – purpose'.

Readers will have realised that hyperthinking is essentially practical thinking, as opposed to ponderous academic thought or pointless blue sky speculation. The core idea of hyperthinking is that intelligence is a tool, not an end in itself; but it all comes to nothing if it is not correctly applied in the real world. This is where the fourth dimension of the theory comes into play – hyperacting.

The real test of the validity of hyperthinking is whether it enables us to generate radical thoughts and ideas that can then be applied in the here and now. It is not about having creative thoughts for their own sake; it is about developing your thinking skills so that you are able to solve problems faster, shift perspectives and generate new ideas that can be introduced into the real world.

I am well aware of the negative connotations of the word hyperacting, but in choosing it I am deliberately seeking to capture the positive emotions, the stimulation, excitement and enthusiasm of the hyperthinker in full flow. So it is not about being hyperactive in the negative sense: everyone has the image of a frenzied child careering about wildly in different directions without purpose. On the contrary, hyperacting is about harnessing precious mental energy and channelling it into what you are doing, applying your ideas with passion and clarity. Hyperacting is, in essence, the application of hyperthinking; it can help you to change and improve a general situation, or solve a particular problem. In order to work it has to be a fluid and dynamically active process in which the hyperthinker makes the *conscious* decision to hyperact – relying on mere spontaneity is only likely to produce another bout of blue sky nonsense that is no use to anyone.

As author and coach Luc Limère likes to say, 'Energy flows where the intention goes', and it is vital for hyperthinkers to focus only on positive things because that is where their energy will flow. If the negativity is allowed to dominate, valuable mental energy will be drawn inexorably towards it and ultimately wasted. This explains why a workplace in which negativity festers unchecked can seem as if it is in a tailspin. Negative emotion feeds on itself, becoming self-fulfilling to such an extent that counteracting what is, in effect, a contamination becomes almost impossible. By remaining visibly positive and upbeat in the face of the severest setbacks hyperthinkers can help prevent this disastrous situation from materialising in the first place, and they can also provide the energy that fuels the forward momentum of good ideas.

Some may allege that the relentless positivity of the hyperthinker is 'inauthentic' and somehow a con trick. I could not disagree more. Hyperthinkers may be innately positive but they accentuate the trait out of necessity. It is, after all, the job of leaders to lead and find solutions: how, exactly, is that to be achieved by people who can only see the negative in a situation? This is not, by the way, a suggestion that hyperthinkers should embrace 'blind optimism', as this can create the delusions that mar much self-improvement literature. Hyperthinkers focus on the positive aspects of a challenging situation, whilst remaining realistic about possible adverse developments. Some call it 'realistic optimism': but however you call it, it enables you to accept that things can go wrong and to prepare for this contingency by building a plan B into your overall plan. In a sense you need to be able to have three thoughts at once when starting a new project: the positive vision of how it could be an incredible success; a realistic backup plan if some things go wrong; and finally a 'paranoid plan' for how to survive if everything that might actually go wrong does indeed go wrong.

But don't think that hyperacting is only suitable for those manic types who walk around grinning 24/7 and never see the downside of anything, although they may find it of use in other respects. In keeping with the supple and malleable nature of hyperthinking, hyperacting will take different forms when used by different people. In certain circumstances the practitioner might be so calm and focused on the matter in hand that they may not appear to be hyperacting at all. Appearances can be deceptive: they are hyperacting all right, but in a way that suits their particular situation – in the office late at night and with a report due the next morning. But that sort of Zen-like calm and focus might be totally unsuited to another situation of greater urgency, one which demands visible energy – perhaps in the form of physical movement, volubility and demonstrable creativity that is protean, shifting and changing as the session unfolds. So although ideas almost always need the energising presence of a dominant personality to drive them forward, it will be seen that hyperacting can be used equally as well by the introvert and extrovert personality. It has numerous manifestations. The simple point to always remember is that hyperacting is the outcome of all that has gone before in terms of hyperthinking and hypershifting. In other words, it is the final capture and application of all that creative thought, energy, emotion and passion.

⑩ Collaboration

Putting these radical new ideas into practice will be a challenge, especially for those working in conservative or risk-averse organisations. This is why hyperthinkers need to find new ways to collaborate, share ideas and spread their values. Creativity and engagement are essentially functions of the individual, but they are also partly created by the surroundings in which the hyperthinker works and the people they work with. Thus far, the main focus of this book has been on what individuals can do to change their mindset as this is the area over which we have most personal and immediate control. We are able to transform a great deal both for ourselves and whatever projects we happen to be working on by improving our mindset. However, when looking at how individuals are able to bring about change in their organisations and society at large, the role of others and of the environment in which we work is critical. In this chapter I will explore how to bring a culture of hyperthinking into your organisation or your team.

When Apple founder Steve Jobs bought Pixar he realised that one of the major problems in the company was the fact that different departments were divided into silos. These departments were located in several separate buildings, and people had little or no interaction with one another across these divisions: in effect, the physical divisions between the departments had created barriers to effective collaboration and creativity. Jobs wasn't having any of this. He decided to move the entire team to one location, and in an unorthodox move (to put it mildly) he also ordered that there would be only one toilet in the centre, forcing everyone to gravitate towards this place at least a few times a day. According to the feedback of the employees – who understandably were not entirely ecstatic at the idea of having to walk up to 15 minutes to reach the loo – they have almost all had what they call 'bathroom moments': essentially a creative encounter where meeting someone from another department produced an acute insight or an idea that they were later able to use, and that had a significant positive impact on their projects and work in general.

We should never underestimate the creative effects of the chance encounter between people. In his TEDTalk (www.ted.com) of 2010 scientist and author Matt Ridley explained that to bring about new ideas you need to get people to meet in informal environments, thus allowing serendipity to bring out the best in people from different professions and different companies who have been thrown together to share ideas. It may not always result in the creation of totally new ideas as such, but the exploration of old ideas from a new angle always has a chance of bringing about one of those crucial 'aha' moments. Experience has shown time and again that teams will be most creative not in brainstorming meetings, but in free and wide-ranging discussions over lunch, during impromptu walks around the corner and during coffee breaks or around the water cooler. It is these informal exchanges that need to be 'enabled'. So it is clear that meeting new people in different circumstances, asking questions and exchanging experiences with each other can deliver new and sometimes transformational insights. The exchange of one object for another is a unique human trait, and it is that exchange that creates new ideas.

The Internet has exponentially increased our ability to collaborate and share ideas. First and most simply, you can share your insights and ideas with people you already know via simple social media tools; and if you wish to collaborate in a more structured way on serious projects, tools such as Yammer (a closed version of Facebook) and Basecamp (a project collaboration tool) are available. I would urge you to explore them. Although when building relationships meeting face to face can play a crucial part in developing mutual trust and understanding, it is important not to underestimate what a virtual team can achieve without that face-to-face interaction. My own company, ZN, was created from day one as a virtual network (in fact the N in ZN stands for 'network'), and over the years I have experimented with how far we could function as a virtual organisation. Interestingly, my original vision of an 'officeless' company failed. It did so for two reasons: first, people in the core team liked and wanted to come together physically. It is a fact that many people like the idea of a workspace that is separate from their home environment. Second, clients needed the reassurance of a physical space to have meetings and to see that the company existed in a tangible way and would 'be around' in the future (although, of course, having an office is in no way a guarantee of financial stability). However, it is worth pointing out that after we moved from an office with several floors to a single floor, where the teams could interact constantly, we experienced a surge in energy and engagement, and we were able to convey better to our clients the competence of our team and the core values of our business culture.

So although some of my ideas failed, on the other hand certain parts of my experiment did in fact work: some of the suppliers that form a key part of our business are widely spread in India, Croatia and the US, but they work as a wholly reliable part of the team thanks to a generous use of Skype and other online collaboration tools. Individual team members also have a high degree of flexibility, and can work from home using Skype and online access – by and large our loose approach seems to work very well.

But when observing online behaviour up close we quickly realise how important virtual identity is becoming, and how effective virtual collaboration can be. Many people argue that a virtual identity somehow counts for less than a physical one. This is, of course, to miss the point entirely. As we saw in the hyperlink chapter, teenagers have now embraced Facebook and regard it as an intrinsic part of their own identities, whether the critics like it or not. In just the same way that how you dress and what you say in public defines how you are perceived by your peers, so your Facebook profile becomes a part of who you are. People *can* engage in deeply emotional relationships on Facebook, as witnessed by the ever-growing number of online romances – even marriage proposals – that have originated on digital networks. This reminds us of the strong and deep emotional bonds that can be created and developed through online channels: teams of friends and business collaborators can have strong loyalties and profoundly understand each other's perspectives through the use of these tools.

When you step back and contemplate the series of happy accidents that led to the birth of the World Wide Web and the unprecedented wave of innovation and collaboration that followed, it merely confirms that virtual collaboration is now possible on a scale never before imagined. The Web has laid the foundation for new ways in which to learn, share knowledge, and also to love and to hate. But the point I wish to make is that it has all been accomplished without a 'master plan' drawn up by a guiding hand, and without a company with deep pockets creating some highly sophisticated code to try to own this new and invaluable piece of real estate. And despite the best efforts of certain companies who are intent on 'owning' the Web, it seems as if they are always vulnerable to the next start-up company that builds an entirely new business model operating according to different rules. Two of the most startlingly successful breakthrough projects to emerge from the Internet are Open Source and Wikipedia. Both share several key features: they are collaborative in nature, and offer something of significant value and for free to the whole of (connected) society. They operate outside the normal commercial paradigms, appear somewhat ludicrously idealistic and were both dismissed as 'impossible dreams' in their early phase. Yet their unparalleled success can teach us all something about a new paradigm of virtual collaboration.

Open Source is a technology that has been developed for free by programmers. They share code with each other and upload new developments which are available for anyone to download and use. All this is done without demanding a fee: the implications and sheer generosity of this are astounding. The people behind the Open Source movement were initially motivated by the ideology of providing free software for the world, but it soon developed into a new culture and a new business model. The important insight provided by this incredible story is that it was unforeseen and unpredictable (one of our black swans, in fact). To understand it requires a paradigm shift away from the conventional theories about programming and copyright that still dominate much of society today. Our past notions are not sufficient to explain how this has been possible. But it is not a free-for-all: collaboration around Open Source is highly sophisticated and regulated. A set of defined rules allows a community of developers to evaluate new code and ensure quality is maintained. Astonishingly, no manager is responsible for this and no one earns money directly through it. The result is an extraordinary resource that continues to improve the foundation of the Web and the experience of the users, as well as further stimulating the creativity of the programmers.

In contrast to the planning that lay behind Open Source, Wikipedia started as an accident. The announcement in March 2012 that the *Encyclopaedia Britannica* was to end its printed version marks the end of an era, and the substitution of an old paradigm for a new one. It is also the end of a struggle between two world views: one symbolised by the *Britannica*, which is the outcome of an editing and publishing process that is marked by authoritative and command-and-control techniques; and the other by Wikipedia, the accidental and haphazard result of an attempt to create a free encyclopedia available to all. As Wikipedia has come out the clear winner from this struggle, it is interesting to look deeper into Wikipedia to see what can be learned from this project in terms of collaboration.

Today Wikipedia consists of almost 4 million articles in English alone, authored by 751,426 contributors; and it has become, for a vast majority of people, the undisputed reference point for settling any questions – ranging from the composition of an atom to the next episode of *Desperate Housewives*. The level of accuracy of Wikipedia has been the subject of much-heated controversy, but after extensive analysis it has been found that on average it is able to deliver the same level of quality as the *Encyclopaedia Britannica*, only with much less cost and more breadth. Wikipedia functions thanks to a network of dedicated volunteers, and just like the Open Source movement they are governed by reasonably precise rules and conventions which allow them to collaborate effectively without needing a financial or organisational incentive. Needless to say, a hyperthinker needs to be constantly exploring these possibilities, and looking to find other hyperthinkers to see if they can leverage the new paradigm to reach their goals and make further discoveries and innovations. They do so by asking themselves what information or network might be available through the Internet that they could connect to in order to achieve their goals.

An important question to ask is what kind of information you can find by searching Google or Wikipedia: will these tools be enough, or do you need to reach further and find informed blogs that might helpfully aggregate relevant information? In this search for information hyperthinkers need to apply a rigorous journalistic and scientific mindset to validating the information they find, always asking questions:

- What is the source of this information, and how can I evaluate the reliability of that source?

- How many corroborating sources can I find to validate it?

- Is it on a known and respected site such as the BBC, *The Economist* or MIT, a site where I can expect that at least some of the fact checking has been done, or do I need to dig deeper until I find additional corroboration for myself?

Second, when a story unfolds, you can search your networks on Facebook, Twitter and LinkedIn to see who can help you validate the story. This happened to me recently when I watched the now famous 'Kony2012' video that appeared on YouTube. Within a few days this video became one of the most successful viral videos of all time, passing through the 100,000,000 view mark. The video told the story of Joseph

Kony, a warlord in Uganda who had been responsible for the abduction of children and the murder of innocent people, as well as innumerable acts of rape and brutality against men, woman and children over the past 30 years. The video called for action, and had been put together by a group calling itself 'Invisible Children'. One of the reasons the video was so appealing is that the storytelling was potent and well executed; it connected to young people in a tremendously effective way. I saw this occur with my own children (aged eight and 12), who watched the video and decided that as a family we should support the campaign. I thought that this would be a good exercise in critical thinking and told them that we could do so, but only after analysing the campaign to examine the story behind it. The campaign had already met a controversial push-back from many groups and sources. People were accusing the organisation 'Invisible Children' of spending too much of their money on making 'cool videos' and not enough on supporting practical activities on the ground. Others claimed that the story oversimplified the situation, and portrayed Uganda, and Africa in general, in a negative light which didn't help people understand the reality of the situation as it actually is.

As I looked at the story unfolding on Facebook and other places online I found that an old friend of mine who had worked with me on the student radio project in Oxford over 15 years before was being interviewed on CNN. He was one of the few reporters who had met with the now infamous warlord and had also written a book about Kony. I trusted my former colleague's judgement, and wanted to know what he thought about the story. As he had gained some minor celebrity status because of the story, many people were discussing things on his Facebook wall. I was confused about the hostility and critical tone of the reviews I was reading, and so I put the following simple question directly to him: 'Do you think I should buy the "action kit" for my kids to support the campaign, or is this a case of misplaced hacktivisim?' His answer, in a nutshell, was yes we should support the campaign, and he expanded upon his point the next day in an article in the *Financial Times*. Basically what he was saying was Kony was an evil warlord who should be stopped. This was undeniable, and despite some oversimplification of the campaign and the questions about the organisation 'Invisible Children', it didn't change the fact that the goal was a good one and justified. During the following days, further stories emerged and developed online, shedding light on the Christian evangelical nature of the organisation and the bizarre mental breakdown of the film-maker behind the video. It turned out that he had struggled to withstand the unexpected scrutiny after the video had become world famous. By this point I felt that it was thanks to some extensive reading and – critically – contacting my network online that I had been able to make an informed judgement. In short, the intention of the campaign was thoroughly laudable, although the nature of the organisation 'Invisible Children' was questionable.

The ability to critically evaluate information needs to be further developed as we become more dependent on fast-flowing information coming from the Internet; and children – as well as adults – need to know how to ensure that they are critically and correctly assessing the information they get from the Web. If you are able to use your networks – from your friends on Facebook to your professional networks – you will be able to get numerous insights and information that can help you make judgements and take important decisions, and get them right. So hyperthinkers invest time and effort in their networks, and use them to gain further understanding of issues or to find talent and help with projects. A smart and systematic use of your networks can turn them into powerful tools. Just as highly connected people have the ability to find help in most situations, so we now have the ability to use a virtual web of contacts to expand our networks all the way around the globe.

So as you start looking at how to approach your next project, look at the information you can find online and critically evaluate it by looking for multiple perspectives, and indeed by hypershifting to look at what you find from different angles – and remember, always check the source of this information: don't be afraid to junk it if it appears dubious. Practice using your networks to get trustworthy help, advice and insights into particular problems; and also use them to find the skills you might need to help you reach your goals. When building a team, look to your colleagues as well as your virtual networks to see who might be able to contribute from anywhere around the globe. And when looking for new ideas, remain open to serendipitous encounters with people in your own office environment as well as online. And finally, radically re-imagine how you might be able to create a team from scratch or draw from an existing pool of talent: remember the power of Wikipedia and Open Source to create new models of collaboration and refuse to be limited by the old paradigms – you too might have the opportunity to create your successful 'Wikiteam'.

PART FOUR

Becoming a Hyperthinker

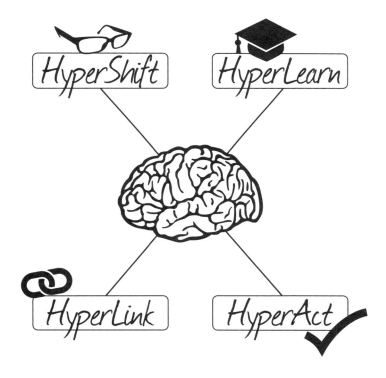

(11) Embarking on the Journey

Having given you an overview of the four dimensions that underpin hyperthinking, let me now turn to how you can apply this to your own life.

The journey towards becoming a hyperthinker will be unique to each individual. You will need to define your own route, but I will put together some suggestions which you can take as inspiration to create your own programme and embark on a journey that will never end. Before going into details about this there are a few commitments that you need to make with yourself.

First, articulate your desire to become a 'hyperthinker'. This will make no assumptions about your current capabilities, but simply helps you to consciously articulate that you want to focus on key aspects of your thinking and learning in order to start a process of ongoing transformation. It means that this is not a one-off effort to try out a technique, but more of a life-changing commitment to take thinking seriously and to start exercising your thinking muscles. It also evokes a dynamic effort that you will ensure this commitment generates concrete results.

Second, you need to accept that applying the principles of hyperthinking takes time, practice and play. It is a sustained and long-term effort to work on your mind and your mental aptitude, anchored in the belief that this focus in itself will be a part of the learning. There is no quick fix, no miracle solution, but a realisation that just as we took time to learn to read and write – we need to time to exercise and develop our thinking muscles. So, decide now that you want to make this change. Decide that you want your mind to evolve to embrace the world around you by understanding it through multiple perspectives.

Hyperthinking is designed to help make explicit what many authors have hinted at without ever having woven it into a single system of thought. The idea of learning how to improve your thinking by concentrating on four key dimensions provides a framework in which to regularly consider your progress. You have the freedom to adapt the framework to what works for you, but having a system that you identify with is the key to helping you sustain this transformation.

The hyperthinking system is designed primarily for people who feel that they need help in structuring something that they see as inherently disorganised. Our culture and society often considers creative people as born with a particular set of skills. For those who don't consider themselves as 'natural creative types', and this covers a large part of the workforce today, the conceptual framework generated by hyperthinking is of enormous help in giving structure and coherent form to these skills.

On the other hand, there are some people who are 'natural' hyperthinkers: people for whom creativity and technology are second nature. For those people this system might seem unnecessary; however, they might also recognise some aspects of the system as useful. Most importantly it could give them a language to communicate with colleagues, friends and family about the skills needed to undertake the projects in which they excel. And I invite them to share and improve the hyperthinking system by adding tools, insights and suggestions that have worked for them. However, as I define a hyperthinker as an ideal state, I am assuming that there is no 'perfect' hyperthinker out there: only people aspiring to improve different aspects of their thinking, and ready to share their experiences with each other. Sharing itself is a tremendous tool for learning, as we will discover later.

Finally, you need to accept that creativity is a learned skill, and the more time and practice you dedicate to this part of your thinking the better you will get at it; and also that the ability to think creatively is a core skill that needs to be developed regardless of profession. I believe that hyperthinking will be to the twenty-first century what reading and writing were to the twentieth century.

The best place to start is to contemplate a full year ahead, and create your own 12-month plan. By doing this you can have your very own learning programme that you can update and refine on a monthly basis, and then renew every year. In the next 12 months select the key skills you want to improve and decide how you will build a routine to acquire these skills; always remain open to change and adjustment. For each month identify the key learning goals you have so that you can track your progress and see how you are improving. When putting your own curriculum together, combine all the learning tools that you can use to acquire the skills: books, audiobooks, podcasts (audio recordings), websites and online groups involved in these particular activities.

Decide on the time you can allocate to this effort, but make sure that it is regular and that it becomes part of your routine. The time you are able to spend on this will vary according to the demands of your professional and personal life, but once you get into the habit of doing this you will see how much it feeds into your activities and helps you to become more productive, more energised and more creative with your existing activities. I would suggest making room for at least 10–15 minutes a day for this activity, which can then expand into longer time slots when possible.

The two aspects of thinking that can help to stretch your mind most are exposure to new perspectives and discovering and using new thinking tools. Hypershifting – finding new perspectives – is the best way to start. This can be done by reading books, watching videos online and listening to podcasts on various subjects.

You should be able to identify many good sources of inspiring videos on the Web by looking at YouTube, iTunes and any other sources that might provide you with great content. TED.com is a great place to get inspired by new perspectives. On this site you will find thousands of videos of short presentations (from a few minutes to their standard 18-minute format) which often give you a striking perspective on something you had never heard of, or a dramatic new insight into something you have taken for granted. If you have a daily routine which involves exercising or travelling by some means that allows you to watch videos, I would suggest that you keep a few slots for one or two videos from this kind of resource. Many other organisations also provide this kind of material, much of which can be found on YouTube (you can check the educational section on youtube.com/education). Google has a regular event called Zeitgeistminds, which compiles a series of TED-like presentations on videos that can be accessed free on YouTube.

Some of the great TEDTalks that have attracted most views are also very good places to start: Ken Robinson on education – giving us a radical insight into what is wrong with our current thinking on education; Jill Bolte Taylor's 'Stroke of Insight' describes the extraordinary story of a neurosurgeon experiencing and surviving a brain seizure. You can also watch an utterly original way to present a physics paper by watching 'Dance your PhD' by Johan Bohannon, and see how *Eat, Pray, Love* author Elizabeth Gilbert gets inspired. These are all videos that will make you think differently about one or several aspects of life.

When you come across something of interest and you wish to deepen your understanding of the topic, google the author of the presentation and check whether they have a website, a book (or an e-book) or perhaps a podcast. This will enable you to dig deeper into a specific perspective and become more acquainted with it. If you feel really interested in something you might want to keep some notes on what was particularly striking about the presentation and the key thoughts you wanted to capture. You can do this using a free online tool like evernote.com (which serves as a notebook across platforms, and even allows you to record voice notes on your mobile phone). Second, you might want to engage with the author by commenting on their blog, tweeting something they are talking about or simply by sending them an email. But to do this you will need to create your own online identity.

To be a part of the great online conversation that is going on you need to spend time creating and maintaining your own online identity and voice. Most people will already have done

one or both of these things, but I would strongly encourage you to ensure that you have an online existence that is easy to find and well maintained – which can mean very different things for different people.

A NEW PERSONA

A lot of people have a negative image of social networks and digital relationships, and perhaps with some justification: we have all read stories of fools getting married on Facebook and divorced two days later. More interesting to me is the discussion going on that claims that having 'friends' on Facebook is less valuable than having friends in real life. It is an argument with some merit, but I heard an interview with an Oxford futurologist in which he stated that this assertion comes from a profound misconception about what we are as human beings. According to this thinker, as human beings we communicate through abstract symbols, spoken words and written words. These form the bonds that we have with other people. We talk to each other and write to each other and thus form relationships. That seems indisputable, and so taking the point to its logical conclusion, whether we perform this activity through digital means that happen to be online or through printed means such as a piece of paper makes absolutely no difference: we are doing the same thing – connecting with other people and having a relationship.

In my view online relationships are every bit as 'real' as those where we have conversations on the phone or face to face. It is important to accept that this is the case. The reason online communication has grown so quickly is not just because it is convenient – it resonates much more deeply with people and their sense of identity. In fact, online tools are changing our notion of what our identity is and can be, and this is sure to enrage certain people. We remain the same physical person, of course, but now we also have the freedom to become an online persona: whether the sober professional person on LinkedIn or the hedonist on Facebook. As Mark Zuckerberg has said, we all have private and professional lives that we can – if we wish – bring together in a new, merged persona. This is a serious step to take, and it could have far-reaching consequences – your reputation will be heavily influenced by what you say online. But this is neither better nor worse than the traditional reputation that you may have created for yourself among your circle of 'real' friends by some ill-advised behaviour on a Friday night after work.

If you do decide to take the step of merging your personas – and I would urge you to do so – then remember that you will be shaped by these online tools, and so you need to start deciding what you think is important, what messages you would like to convey and how you would like to be seen. Just as you would in 'real' life: see – it's not so different.

Creating a business profile on LinkedIn or one of the other business networks has now become crucial for professionals who want to build their networks. It is also an insurance policy in case one day you need to change jobs. It will enable you to start growing your network and have active conversations with people who might be able to find your next opportunity. Make sure your professional profile is up to date, and start connecting with other professionals. Remember that when someone visits your LinkedIn profile they can immediately make out your level of comfort with technology and the Internet by seeing how well you have created your profile. Second, I would suggest having a presence on Facebook, whether you choose to share a little or a lot with the world, simply so that you are able to understand the dynamics of the network and engage with various other people with whom you might not otherwise connect. Facebook is increasingly blurring the boundaries between professional and private lives, and you need to see how both fit together. Then you can use tools such as Twitter to observe what other people are saying, and perhaps share interesting links with people who choose to follow you.

One assumption you must make at all times when communicating online – be it by email, on Facebook, LinkedIn, Twitter or any other channel – is that what you write and share is never fully private, even if it is supposed to be (never believe your privacy settings). This means that you need to think carefully about what would happen if the comment, photo or video you are uploading were to end up in front of the person that you would least like to see it. Keep that uppermost in your mind and you cannot really go wrong. But be aware that information online can and often does end up in front of the people you are trying to hide it from.

The next phase of developing your professional identity is to decide how you want to share information: for example whether you want to share through a platform such as a blog or Google+ that enables you to write longer content than that which appears on platforms such as Twitter; or whether you want to use multiple channels to communicate simultaneously.

You need to remember that you should never let the technology control you. You can always take steps to decide how much time each platform you are testing needs, but don't be afraid to let go of a platform that doesn't work for you. And don't feel that simply because you have set up an account with Twitter or Facebook you now need to spend hours on it every day. The best approach to this is to test things out with a step-by-step approach, and find the kind of content that works for you. You might limit yourself to sharing short one-liners through Twitter (140 characters or less), or you may want to use video or podcasting if you find that you feel more comfortable with these media. As new tools keep coming along you should make a point of testing them and discard the ones that don't work for you. Eventually you will end up with a number of different profiles online, and some preferred channels to tell your own individual story. Even if you choose to limit your conversation online, you will at least have direct experience of the different channels available; and the very attempt to experience a new channel will have provided you with new learning opportunities.

Now that you have started hypershifting by exploring new perspectives and hyperlinking by creating your online identity, you can start developing your creativity toolkit and get hyperlearning. You can develop your thinking skills using the abundant literature and vast array of practical tools that are available, but you do need to choose. As indicated in Chapter 7, I recommend becoming familiar with Edward de Bono, who provides much of the theoretical foundation behind creative thinking: look at the different tools that can be found in his many books (*Six Thinking Hats* and *Six Action Shoes* are two of my personal favourites).[1]

I also suggest becoming a regular user of mind mapping: both the technique and the software can enable you to visualise your thoughts and organise your ideas in a visual and intuitive way. My personal experience suggests that when introducing this to people it can very quickly become habitual without the need for much training. However, I would also suggest that some background reading about the concept would be helpful. In his excellent book *Thinking for a Change*, Michael Gelb shows how this technique can help with creative thinking.[2] You can supplement this reading by checking out the numerous videos on the subject that you can find online; it will all help you to discover the best applications for you.

There are thousands of websites on the subject, and many people spend time categorising different techniques and

---

1 Edward de Bono, *Six Thinking Hats* (Boston, MA: Little, Brown, 1985); *Six Action Shoes* (New York: HarperBusiness, 1991).
2 Michael Gelb, *Thinking for a Change: Discovering the Power to Create, Communicate and Lead* (London: Aurum, 1996).

offering very useful guidance on new techniques: their feedback on what works and what doesn't is a fantastic resource. As ever with the danger of information overload you must choose what you think will work for you. Check through the references in books by the authors you already trust and decide which new techniques you should try.

There are many websites that I find particularly useful when it comes to actively hyperlearning new tools. Litemind.com is good example of a website that reviews interesting tools and books on creativity and productivity. The website's creator and author, Brazilian Luciano Passuello, has compiled many resources on the subject of improving the mind. He even offers a free e-book with a summary of some of the best techniques he has come across over the years. He also publishes a blog which gives up-to-date insights into new techniques he has discovered and tested. It is well worth reading Passuello and keeping up with his thoughts.

You can also visit Iqmatrix.com for some inspiring mind maps of authors and concepts. This company provides an array of material on a variety of learning concepts and tools. The authors have compiled mind maps that can be printed on people such as Steve Jobs, Einstein and Walt Disney, but they also deal with topics such as Thinking Hats, how to use Twitter or how to overcome obstacles. Most of the maps are available free in PDF format, but larger posters can be purchased on the site. I find that printing the occasional map from the site can serve as a useful reminder of breakthrough ideas, so it is worth having them around from time to time.

Exploring these sites and listening to related podcasts or audiobooks on the subject of creativity should be fully integrated in your hyperthinking routine. But having said that, I would exercise a note of caution here as none of these techniques are magic bullets, and much of this literature has a tendency to oversell itself. There are insights, new perspectives and new tools that can be found from exploring and testing these ideas, but approach them without assuming that any of them provides a final answer or a definitive guide to improving your mind. Conceive of them simply as new 'exercise routines' that can help expand your abilities and perspectives, but always continue your journey of exploring and testing to see how new tools and techniques might capture something that could be of use to you.

There are also sites that offer excellent learning material in more traditional subjects. These range from the section on education that can be found in iTunes (iTunes U) to the education section of YouTube. In addition, there are several sites dedicated to online learning, such as the Khanacademy. org and udemy.com. These sites give you access to a range of courses on an almost unlimited number of subjects. I would suggest that you pick subjects of most interest to you – maybe topics that you found fascinating at school or university but didn't get a chance to pursue – or simply something that you would like to include in your learning routine. This keeps your mind firmly in learning mode, and will serve as a reminder that learning never ends. Revisiting topics that you have already studied before, and combining this with your subsequent life experience, is also a way to prevent your thinking from going stale. It links the new concepts you have discovered with older base knowledge, thereby making new and potentially fruitful connections.

Although I have made some specific suggestions in this chapter, they are only there to get you started and enable you to create the flow and selection of relevant content that works for you.

Once you are exposed to new tools, new perspectives and new ideas you will find that by sharing this experience with friends or colleagues it will stimulate you further to investigate, reflect and deepen your understanding of your discoveries. I suggest that you take the lead in forming a network of people that can meet on a regular basis (monthly perhaps) to discuss what you have learned and how it has helped you. You can continue and broaden your conversations through online groups: yammer. com, mentioned earlier, is a very convenient platform for having discussions with small or large groups of people; but Facebook, Google+ and others all offer ways to quickly and simply share online knowledge. This will help you to properly evaluate and challenge the knowledge that you discover.

As soon as you begin the hyperlearning process and get your brain in gear for learning about the extraordinary opportunities around you, always look for chances to apply that new-found creativity. As well as forming your own chapter of hyperthinkers, join other local networks of fellow professionals or interesting people that you can use to meet new people, get new ideas and change perspectives. TED.com has a network of TEDx franchises that represent smaller (and cheaper) versions of the global organisation where people come together for a day to share ideas following some of the guidelines of the TED.com global event. I was personally involved with the set-up and launch of TEDxBrussels, and saw at first hand how such a radical concept could be introduced in a city often seen as rather uninspired and conservative. The first event took place in the European Parliament, which proved – if nothing else – that it could be done in the heart of one of the most bureaucratic organisations on earth. You can decide to join or even start your own TEDx in your locality. This could be a great opportunity for you to meet like-minded people, and just by virtue of taking the initiative you start changing things around you.

As you move from the safer 'theoretical' learning part of hyperthinking to the practical, highly engaged hyperacting part, you will need to be flexible, comfortable with change and ready to accept small failures, as these minor setbacks will form the backbone of your learning. When you embrace an ambitious project that requires you and your team to venture into the unknown there will always be a certain amount of risk – and with that comes an element of possible failure. Being able to learn from and recover from failure quickly is a core characteristic of hyperthinking. We should not be paralysed by new ideas; rather we should become very good at testing, adapting and discarding ideas so that we eventually find the good one. Remember that Thomas Edison tested over 10,000 light bulbs before finding one that worked, and we should not be afraid of a failing a few hundred times before getting it right.

So start now by deciding that you want to embark on this journey towards becoming a hyperthinker: create your plan and keep your brain open to new perceptions, new ideas and new thinking tools. You will find that, as with many things, the journey – not the destination – is its own reward.

⑫ (Almost) the Final Word

*Here's to the crazy ones. The misfits. The rebels. The
trouble-makers. The round pegs in the square holes.
The ones who see things differently. They're not fond
of rules, and they have no respect for the status quo.
You can quote them, disagree with them, glorify, or
vilify them. But the only thing you can't do is ignore
them. Because they change things. They push the
human race forward. And while some may see them
as the crazy ones, we see genius. Because the people
who are crazy enough to think they can change the
world, are the ones who do.*

Think Different – *Apple campaign, 1997*

Hyperthinkers are people who want to change the world by
adapting their own individual mindsets to the new realities
of our times. It is the convergence of these two intellectual
currents that makes the hyperthinking idea so powerful:
accepting reality in order to change it. As we have come to
see the twenty-first century as the beginning of a new era
characterised by permanent change, many of us have felt
confused and deeply troubled, fearing that these changes
might impose heavy demands upon us that are far beyond our

capabilities to cope with. But I have argued that when looking at the incredible opportunities that these changes represent for us as individuals, we can step back and start to see that by radically changing our mindset we can embrace this changed world and start transforming it: we can, in short, become actors in the great events that are unfolding instead of merely impotent spectators gawping hopelessly on the sidelines.

Becoming a hyperthinker is first and foremost about deciding to adapt your thinking to this new environment. By making this initial decision change will then start to occur naturally. But as with every true learning experience it will involve a certain amount of struggle; you will have to learn to live outside your comfort zone. But persevere and the rewards can be great. When learning and experimentation becomes second nature we are able to reconnect to an early stage of our lives when everything was new – when we were able to gaze in wonder at the extraordinary achievements and feats of invention made by humankind, and marvel at how exciting and challenging everything in nature can appear. We have so much to learn, and because of the fact that we are only at the beginning of this transformation *we* can be the pioneers and architects of this new world; we just need to make the right choice. The hyperthinker label is meant to make this decision easier, and give intellectual clarity and definition to a hazy intuition that many of us have. By using a thinking system that will sharpen our ability to hypershift; creating a permanent hyperlearning programme; hyperlinking with new technology at every opportunity; and hyperacting to test these new ideas at home and at work we can – and will – transform our lives. And the simple and inclusive language of hyperthinking will enable you to share your experiences with others.

Maintaining the mental habits and exercises suggested in this book will be critical to making your mind fitter and more agile: your goal is to remain on a constant learning path. Remember to constantly ask questions about what you are doing, why you are doing it and how things work – or don't work. Learn to be the one in the business meeting who is brave enough to ask the questions that might seem embarrassing. Encourage your colleagues, friends and children to be the same, fearlessly asking questions that others deem foolish – that incessant probing is probably the single most important skill that you can develop in order to sustain you on your hyperthinking journey.

A second habit that you must develop is learning to stay longer with the problems you encounter. The more you are able to find a few minutes where you allow yourself to look for a solution – even for what might turn out to be an unsolvable problem – the more your mind will expand and you will increase your ability to seek and find new solutions. Above all, don't just give up for lack of patience if things don't come quickly. Make this quizzical approach to problems a daily habit, one additional minute at a time.

Third, always remember to be looking for *solutions* whenever you face a difficult problem or a challenge, and sustain that frame of mind throughout the time that you are dealing with the situation. Don't dwell on what goes wrong, or has gone wrong, or lament why some apparently insurmountable problem has landed on your doorstep; rather, discipline your mind to start exploring possible solutions, however difficult or unrealistic this first appears. Always assume and insist to yourself and others that there is a solution that has been overlooked; tell yourself that there is a brilliant answer out there and you will be the one find it. Use the spring of creativity that hyperthinking will inevitably release to link apparently disconnected and random thoughts and ideas. My view is that with this approach you will invent new and dazzling outcomes as a result.

And remain a 'realistic optimist'. As I have stressed many times throughout this book, hyperthinking requires an unswervingly positive attitude in order to be able to look for solutions constantly, and to persevere and cope with setbacks. But this mindset also needs to be balanced by the ability to think of a Plan B, to contemplate the worst case scenario and have solutions for this eventuality in the back of your mind. You need to learn and master these mental gymnastics so that whenever you embark on a new project, you are able to build a positive vision while maintaining contingency plans.

These simple habits can help you to undergo a transformation that will be ongoing. At the same time as you apply these new ideas, revisit regularly the four dimensions of hyperthinking that I have described, and refine the particular meanings that they have for you; see how these dimensions have helped you to generate new perceptions, new ideas and find new solutions. Make hypershifting a part of your life by regularly shifting perspectives and looking at the world through the eyes of total strangers. Challenge your preconceptions about everything, and remember how mistaken even the most intelligent people have been in the past. Believing in our preconceptions is our default position. There is nothing wrong with this if you can also remember that our assumptions can, and often are, deeply flawed. Embark on the hyperlearning journey by going back to 'school'. But this time you get to design a school that is tailor-made by and for you. Combining the subjects and techniques that you want to learn with the unlimited reach of the Internet gives you access to new knowledge, ideas and people

– something that was unimaginable only a few years ago. And, of course, overcome any resistance to and reservations that you may have had about technology, and embrace its true magic and fun by hyperlinking. Learn to play, and discover that messing about with technological innovations is a simple pleasure in itself; exploring the practical applications that technology might have for your work and life is a bonus.

Finally, don't forget to hyperact by putting into practice your new ideas, testing them in the real world, at work and with your clients: do so with a new and bold pioneering spirit. Once you choose to become the doer, I am convinced that others will notice and they will rally around you and follow your lead. And if they don't follow you, well then so be it. Build your own path regardless; the loss will be theirs.

The ultimate purpose of this book has been to capture the idea that we need to adapt our mindset to the unavoidable economic and political turbulence of the times that we live in. To do so I used one of the most powerful tools at my disposal: I coined a new word. I make no claim that this word is defined with a scientific rigour (which word is?), only that it can help reshape our perception and motivate us to learn something new and useful every day. It is also designed to break some of the myths that hold us back – myths that have some of us believing that we can never be really creative, that technology is difficult and that learning is best done in a school. By destroying these myths and embracing a new, more flexible, more positive and more open mindset we can 'reboot' our brains.

The word 'hyperthinker' is, of course, just a simple trick. It is designed to convince you that it is possible to change, to learn and to adapt yourself to the new conditions by embracing certain concepts. If you can fool your mind into believing that you are a hyperthinker, then by making the time for learning, experimentation and trial and error you will make your personal transformation real, since it is ultimately your mind that determines your mindset.

Many of the concepts and insights outlined in this book are by and large well known and documented. However, merely reading a book or listening to a presentation about change will only help us start to adapt our outlook: it won't finish the job. It is only with the conscious decision to change and the application of the key steps outlined earlier that change can start and then, crucially, be sustained. The 'hyperthinker' concept serves as a reminder of the ongoing process that we need to engage with. Personally speaking, it helps me to remember to pick up a new book, to watch a new and inspiring video, or learn a new skill simply to keep my mind fit. It helps me to remain curious instead of complacent and, like the slave whispering 'Remember you are mortal' in the Roman general's ear, it always reminds me of how little I actually know about most things.

Recently I received an email from someone who wanted advice on finding work in Brussels. She lived abroad and had just finished her studies. Having recently drafted several chapters of this book, and with the ideas fresh in mind, I decided to call her back. After listening to her I outlined some of the steps I had just written about. She told me later that she had been completely inspired by the conversation, and reading early drafts of the book had given her boundless energy and motivation. She had immediately set to work realising her plan and was reinventing an online persona that would tell her story and expand her network of contacts. From time to time I still get feedback either face to face or by email about how the hyperthinking concept resonated with her. It is clear that this simple word tapped into something that she knew intuitively but had never articulated. It helped her to build a structured approach to a journey into a new and unknown intellectual environment. I am hoping that this book can – and will – do the same for you. I hope that it will help you to step back from your everyday activity and look at the world with a fresh and revealing perspective. I hope that it will help you rediscover the joy of learning simple things, of asking basic questions without fear of being defined as ignorant; and I hope that it will inspire you to face the occasional failure without being defined by others as a failure. And I am not here to claim that I alone have found the secret formula for success; on the contrary, I hope that *you* can help *me* improve on the idea of hyperthinking: together I am convinced that we can make this remarkable thinking tool even better.

> *Life can be much broader once you discover one simple fact, and that is – everything around you that you call life, was made up by people that were no smarter than you. And you can change it, you can influence it, you can build your own things that other people can use. The minute that you understand that you can poke life and actually something will, you know if you push in, something will pop out the other side, that you can change it, you can mold it. That's maybe the most important thing. It's to shake off this erroneous notion that life is there and you're just gonna live in it, versus embrace it, change it, improve it, make your mark upon it. (Steve Jobs, 1994)*

125

PART FIVE

Stories of Hyperthinking

⑬ Meet the Real Hyperthinkers

Anyone and everyone can become a hyperthinker.

Many people have done exceptional things that have stemmed from flashes of insight and inspiration that could legitimately be described as hyperthinking. This book has tried to find an all-encompassing word to describe this thread running across and through these different thoughts and actions, so that it will hopefully become easier to understand and replicate this behaviour. In this chapter I want to share some stories of individuals that illustrate one or more aspects of hyperthinking. The people I will speak about were not necessarily consciously aware of hyperthinking as a concept when they achieved their particular success, but their stories help to illustrate how I have come to formulate the concept and what I mean by it. The experience some have had clearly shows how thinking differently and creatively allowed them to transform a situation using some of the ideas, tools and techniques I have gathered together in this book. So who are these real hyperthinkers?

Ian Andersen works in the Interpretation Department of the European Commission. His job title is External Communications Adviser, a description that wouldn't mean much to most people, and might raise some sceptical eyebrows from those who might be familiar with many of the European Union's (EU's) ponderous and long-winded communications initiatives. The European Commission has faced its fair share of challenges in trying to communicate its messages, and attempts to reach out to European citizens have, by and large, not been successful. It has created a long and cumbersome process to create new communication programmes that has had a tendency to limit innovation and has created very little impact. This has made the Commission famous (one might almost say infamous) for launching strange and bizarre initiatives that get exposure for all the wrong reasons: as is well-known, the press has a field day with much of this. Part of the explanation behind this self-evident failure stems from the bureaucratic culture and rigid paradigm that prevails throughout the institution today. However, even in organisations as large and seemingly inflexible as the EU individuals can still make a profound difference.

Ian's story is – even by the standards of some of the hyperthinkers you will meet here – somewhat unusual. He joined the Commission after a series of serendipitous events that led him to study Chinese, travel around the world and finally end up for personal reasons deciding that his calling was to work in Directorate-General (DG) Interpretation at the EC. He told me that what inspired him initially to follow this unconventional career path started whilst he was biking in his Danish homeland: from out of nowhere he heard a voice calling on him to study Chinese. Well what could he do after something as bizarre as that but promptly accept that it was his fate and pursue this rather unexpected course of action.

After moving restlessly around the world for some time, living in China and other places, he finally arrived at the European

Commission where, after several years, he was tasked with promoting the Interpretation Department, which at that time was facing a major challenge. Not enough qualified young people were learning languages and studying interpreting, which, it was predicted, would eventually lead to a shortfall in graduates able act as interpreters at the myriad conferences and meetings that take place at the EU institutions on a daily basis. To address this future shortfall Ian decided to look at the source of the problem: how could he encourage more students to study interpreting at a time when jobs such as these were becoming increasingly less appealing to a youthful population more drawn by alternative, and apparently much more lucrative, career paths.

Step one was a small experiment in Latvia, where one awareness-raising video uploaded to university websites attracted a great deal of interest from young people, and had quadrupled the number and doubled the quality of applicants to the interpreting MA at Riga University. He decided to delve deeper into this phenomenon, and began to realise that it was a 'no brainer': to engage young people and encourage them in the study of foreign languages and interpreting he needed to engage with them by using the tools that they were using – in other words Facebook and YouTube. Armed with this insight he went on to construct a guerilla marketing campaign, filming events, interviewing candidates for posts as well as people who were already working as interpreters about the benefits of working in this field. The YouTube channel and Facebook group he instigated took off and have become an intrinsic part of every communication effort the Interpretation Department has made since then. At the time of writing there are over 25,000 people who follow the group.

Step two was a test of campaigning in the Czech Republic with a combination of speaking tours and media exposure which proved to have a significant impact on university applications in that country by also reaching the key influencers of the students – their parents and teachers. Thus armed, he established comprehensive standard 'country communication plans' that were rolled out successfully in support of application processes at individual universities in Member States with potential future recruitment issues. All this at minimum cost to the European Commission.

It is important to note that several elements, recognisable as characteristic of hyperthinking, defined Ian's approach. The first thing to mention is that, unlike most other EU-funded projects, he didn't start with a long and complex document defining what was needed – partly because he wasn't sure at the outset of the answer to this. He started by simply experimenting here and there. He found resources inside his team, and was able to allocate the time of some of his interpreter colleagues to filming low-cost videos. He also acted without waiting for the institutions to set up their guidelines for dealing with social media (a grindingly slow process that is, remarkably, still in progress at this moment in time); and, even more interestingly, he single-handedly created a position to run the project for himself, first by defining what needed to be done and then by describing a profile to fill the position – which by a happy coincidence happened to fit his very own professional profile. Ian took this proposition to his boss, who was happy to support him in moving into this new position. As mentioned before in this book, a hyperthinker is someone who doesn't passively wait for events to happen, but rather will seek to take the initiative to change their environment. In several other cases I have observed people replicate Ian's behaviour by seizing the initiative to create their own job description to do what they believed made sense, instead of waiting for someone else to dream up something for them to do.

The second thing to note is that Ian experimented freely instead of overplanning and overtheorising, and he found resources where others often saw none. Third, rather than proceed through the long and complex process of creating a budget for a large EU project, he made things happen by reallocating minor amounts of time and money to his project. The whole campaign was a breakthrough success which landed Ian several communication awards from the International Association of Business Communicators. Perhaps more importantly, it also delivered significantly more impressive results than other similarly ambitious initiatives that were backed by much bigger budgets but that somehow failed to make an impact. Ian is now exploring how to help train over 1,000 communicators from the EU to do things differently and creatively. Still without a predefined framework and restrictive guidelines, Ian continues to shape events as he thinks they need to evolve – and all of this despite operating in an EU framework that many see as rigid and inflexible. For those with some experience of the stifling nature of the EU this is a rare talent and spirited triumph, and Ian seems confident in his abilities to further move a large and lumbering machine in a new direction, one step at a time.

The story of Aurélie Valtat that I told at the beginning of this book is similar to Ian's: she too showed how an individual was able to get a large and complex organisation to embrace social media and engage the full range of communications channels at a time of crisis. Aurélie demonstrated to everyone that even in the most unpromising of circumstances such change *is* possible, and largely boils down to a capable individual seizing the opportunity when it presents itself. Other individuals, however, are able to create the opportunity in the first place.

The educational world, which I described in a negative light earlier when outlining the hyperlearning dimension, is thankfully now being revitalised and has seen new energy in the form of some exciting initiatives. Apple have entered the market with iTunes U, and have reinvented the textbook on the iPad; YouTube and TED as well have helped create a new impetus for learning initiatives, and there is a great deal to be optimistic about when looking at the possibilities unfolding in the educational space. The dominant paradigm that has done so much damage is being challenged – I am certain it cannot hold sway for much longer.

One individual who best illustrates this paradigm shift in educational methods is Salman Khan. A US citizen of Indian origin, he was born and raised in Chicago and started his career as a hedge fund analyst. At one point he was spending time tutoring his young cousin Nadia, who needed help in mathematics. As they lived in different cities, Salman started to record short videos on YouTube to help her with some of her homework. Nadia, joined by some other cousins who had also watched the videos, told Salman that they enjoyed his virtual teaching more than his actual teaching they received at school. This made him pause – he was slightly offended at first – but then after hypershifting and looking at things from their perspective, he understood that his cousins found it easier to listen to him at their own pace, to pause the tape when required and start from the beginning as many times as was needed to understand the subject. All this was possible without his getting frustrated by their taking time to understand what he was explaining. Think of how this compares to what so often happens within the traditional educational structure: facing a difficult subject, and aware that because they don't understand they are causing their tutor to become increasingly frustrated, students become reluctant to ask questions. The result is that the learning process slows and eventually ceases, and everyone leaves feeling thoroughly dissatisfied.

As Salman uploaded these videos and made them public – as he saw no reason not to – he witnessed a strange phenomenon. He found that the videos were being watched by others, who were writing increasingly enthusiastic feedback about them. He made a second hypershift: this way of teaching was scalable, and what was more it was scalable at almost zero additional cost. Every video he uploaded on YouTube could be shared by as many students as could be found, as many times as desired; and they could stay available for others to use for as long as he wanted – all this for no extra cost. As the project started to grow in importance, Salman gave up his day job and created an organisation to develop his project. He started to create a gaming approach which could be used by educators (this radical approach meant that the term could include parents, friends and relatives as well as professional teachers) and students to track their progress in maths by earning badges and increasing their scores. I tested this myself alongside my children, and found that it was a great way to engage with a whole range of subjects without feeling any of the pressure normally associated with an academic environment. The only challenge I felt was that which we feel when gaming and learning.

At a particular TED conference where Salman presented his story he met with Bill Gates, who decided to put some support and cash behind the project. It is clear that this extraordinary initiative could play a major role in how our children learn tomorrow – today. It is also a great place to get our own minds 'back to school' and facing the subjects we never really understood – if for no other reason than just for the sake of keeping our minds in shape.

I have mentioned TED several times in this book as I feel that as a concept it embodies much of the spirit of hyperthinking. The current 'curator', Chris Anderson, has also displayed some outstanding breakthrough hyperthinking. When he became curator of the event, TED was mostly a closed conference, reserved for the technology elite of the West Coast of the US, and attracting other similar sorts from around the world in small numbers. Thus it was highly regarded in the industry but wasn't known much beyond the world of the tech elite. In June 2006, however, a few years after changing the mission of TED to 'ideas worth sharing', Chris made a radical step: he decided to upload videos of all TED presentations online and make them available to the world for free. As the videos started to be uploaded, something unexpected happened. People around the world became captivated by some of these now legendary 18-minute presentations – and these were not about dancing cats and laughing babies. These were intelligent, sometimes complex talks on a wide range of subjects, from philosophy to science, art and history. Some of these talks attracted millions of views, and started to make the brand of TED much better known around the world. Not content with this, Chris then took another bold, some might say slightly deranged step. He gave away the TED brand. He did so by creating TEDx. TEDx is an event that is connected to TED, but it can be run by any individual or group, located anywhere in the world, who requests a licence to run such an event. It brings people together who want to share inspiring ideas and listen to presentations that are in line with the TED philosophy and its values.

Needless to say, this sort of radical thinking was much to my liking. A few years ago I was introduced to a group of people – mainly TEDsters – who wanted to launch TEDx in Brussels, following Chris's vision of creating local versions of the

TED franchise. I was fortunate to see this grow from an idea into one of the most exciting and innovative gatherings in Brussels. The team leading the project was a highly dynamic husband and wife – Walter and Samia. Walter de Brouwer was the thinker and visionary with an extraordinary address book. He had extensive business and academic experience (he is also the CEO of Scanadu and of One Laptop Per Child Europe); and was able to walk into the first meeting with a long and impressive list of speakers who had agreed to join the event and speak. Samia Lounis played the role of chief doer: she was focused on 'making it all happen' despite an extremely tight schedule, no funding to start with and no prior experience in running such large-scale events.

This combination of hyperthinking and hyperacting worked fantastically well for Walter and Samia, and shows how people with complementary skills can come together to achieve great things. Samia told me that on many of the projects they had worked on in the past they had found this role allocation intuitive, and had managed to complement each other by focussing on their own core strengths. Walter's role was to push the boundaries of what could be done (choosing to host the first event in the European Parliament complete with a band, sound and light and high production values was an indication of his vaulting ambition in this respect). He displayed little fear or concern when things went wrong, and kept raising the bar when it came to thinking of new ways to raise the profile of the event, challenging everyone involved to do more and better. Samia, on the other hand, was the pragmatist who looked at every challenge as a list of 'to dos' that needed to get done; her fierce determination and innate talents alone enabled her to succeed. Using his network of contacts and inspirational leadership, and her hard work and organisational genius, Walter and Samia were able to pull off this seemingly impossible scheme, and it became arguably one of the most successful TEDx in the world.

Walter then followed this by experimenting with TEDxKids, a new format designed to give children the 'educational experience of a lifetime'. Again the concept seemed far-fetched and ambitious when I first heard about it, but as the project came together it became a reality that far surpassed the expectations of those involved. My own son was lucky enough to be amongst the 50 children who attended, and to him – and me – it was what school should really be like. To this day he is still using the ideas, tools and insights that he learnt on that day.

In the corporate world hyperthinking is both a necessity and a risk. It means standing out and being the one who tries new things and takes the first steps into the unknown. During the H1N1 crisis ZN was approached by a number of organisations and companies involved in vaccine-related issues to explore what role the Internet was playing in shaping the crisis; or, more accurately as it turned out, how the Web spun the crisis almost out of control. After doing some research looking at what was being said online about vaccines, and who was saying it, we helped the industry shape a new strategy to communicate the truth about H1N1 and vaccination in general using blogs, Twitter, YouTube and other unorthodox channels that usually make every legal department in every pharmaceutical company (rightly) nervous. We met some very interesting people along the way.

Angus Thomson, an Australian with a PhD in molecular biology and a black belt in aikido, was introduced to us in the midst of these projects. As Director of Vaccination Advocacy at Sanofi Pasteur, he quickly embraced the idea of the need for change in his company with enthusiasm and diligence, and started trying to understand how the company had to engage with the world in a different way and rethink its approach to communication. His boundless energy and open mindset has helped to start a new culture in the organisation, which is now experimenting with a series of pilot projects to engage with the public health community and the general public in an open and creative way. Angus firmly believes that his company, and many others in the industry for that matter, needs to accept that the dominant command-and-control paradigm of the twentieth century is now defunct, and that a complete change is needed. This entails a new approach to open communication, learning to let go of the urge to control, and recognising the real concerns of people about certain aspects of healthcare such as vaccination. Instead of the usual – and inadequate – broadcast of scientific facts, a real dialogue has to start about the role of vaccines in society using different, innovative tools (if you still think of social media as innovative, which really you shouldn't).

On Angus's LinkedIn profile you can read the following words of wisdom:

> *We all see the world through our own lenses. Whether as a scientist (been that), parent (am that), national of a country (twice that), male or female (former) … well, you get the idea. Other filters include language (speak 3), culture, generation, emotional state, personal history, and brain hard wiring (not as hard as you think!). In two words: perception = reality. My goal is to understand these filters to improve people's decisions about public health. And maybe life.*

He has already started an honest public discussion about the huge mistakes and choices the health community made when faced with people's misunderstandings about vaccines. Angus has got it: he completely understands the importance of health professionals shifting their mindsets if they are to re-engage with society at large and convince people of the positive role vaccines play in bringing massive health benefits to the population. He talks about real open dialogue, acknowledging difficult issues and the limitations of the industry; he is seeking nothing less than a new language with which to move his profession forward from past mistakes.

When Aurélie Valtat started her online communication 'improvisation' she was careful to communicate to her colleagues – when she found a spare five minutes to do so – how this was helping with the efforts they were all making to address the situation. Twitter became a tool not just to reach and inform the public, but also a powerful component of the official press communications issued by Eurocontrol. Without planning or foresight, one might almost say naturally, this ostensibly trivial technological toy used by inveterate gossips and bores who like the sound of their own voices quickly became an intrinsic part of press briefings, and Aurélie would join in and frantically tweet the latest news to her growing army of followers. This all contributed to her organisation slowly starting to understand the value of these tools. Had she asked permission to do all of this in advance, it would have been denied simply out of fear of the unknown consequences. But once she took the initiative and started, and was able to demonstrate beyond all doubt the benefits of what she was doing, people quickly saw that this was more than a simple technological gimmick.

From this experience Aurélie has learnt about the value of improvisation, enthusiasm, seizing the moment and using technology in a creative and effective way. When she left Eurocontrol to join the European Council – where she faced a challenge of an altogether different level of magnitude – she left behind an organisation that was open to using these new technologies, and a widespread understanding of the fact that they can be *productively* used: they are not just an excuse to waste time at work, the charge so often levelled against them by critics. However, whether this can really continue without the singular energy and particular mindset that she brought to the table is another question; already some of her bolder initiatives are apparently being rolled back. 'It's difficult for people to go as far as we did during the crisis', she told me a few months after leaving for her new job. 'Although the organisation was convinced about the benefits of this radical new communication approach, it takes persistence and continued innovation to really embed it in the culture and the DNA of the organisation. This might still happen at Eurocontrol – but it needs real energy for inertia and entropy not to kick in'. So be under no illusions: bringing about change through hyperthinking is not a simple and easy job. Every day it will require determination and persistence, and the ability to overcome daily setbacks.

The stories I have covered in this chapter illustrate the fact that there are common features to the successful application of hyperthinking in real-life situations. There are many lessons which we can take from these real-life hyperthinkers. *You* need to take the initiative to solve a problem or meet a need you perceive is not being met – no one will do it for you, as Ian showed us with his social media campaign for the EU Interpretation Department. *You* need to be unafraid to venture into uncharted territory and take some measure of personal risk, as Aurélie did during the ash cloud crisis or Walter did with his vision of TEDxBrussels. Technology will play a critical part in your success as you will need to be able to leverage the new tools that have emerged from the 'web soup', as Salman Khan did when his simple but brilliantly effective use of YouTube started to change education as we know it. You cannot always follow a clearly defined plan, and you will need to experiment with improvisation and execute your ideas with gusto, as Samia did when she made the vision of her husband Walter a reality.

By applying hyperthinking to every new challenge you encounter, and always being on the lookout for new perspectives to map out a future you want to see happen; by learning from other like-minded people and gaining the confidence that it can be done, you can become a hyperthinker and join other hyperthinkers in making the world a more exciting place – a place where change is fearlessly embraced, radical solutions to difficult problems are found and new paradigms are endlessly created.

⑭ Catching up with Paul

Paul had gone back home after the final warning from his boss, Pamela, feeling very depressed. As well as feeling miserable about the situation he was supposed to be dealing with, there was no denying that he felt threatened by Pamela: she was young, attractive, highly ambitious and driven – a bit scary, in fact.

Depression gave way to irritation and then raw anger, but that quickly subsided until Paul was left feeling totally overwhelmed and out of his depth. He simply had no idea where to start; how could he, when he did not feel that he understood what he was supposed to be doing. He had spent late nights on Google, and had nearly blurred his vision as he doggedly ploughed through endless terrifying articles about how bad things could get for companies facing crises generated through social media. He had been profoundly affected by this stuff and was starting to wonder if it really was the beginning of the end of the company, let alone himself. With an effort of will he forced himself to try to understand how best to approach the problem. He sensed that there were things that could be done, but his mind churned over and over, and he could not focus. Eventually he settled down in front of the TV with a couple of beers to watch football. It did not help, and the rest of the evening turned out badly: he had an argument with his wife, barked at his kids and began to wonder whether tomorrow really would be his last working day. Finally, he stalked off to bed and suffered a tormented and largely sleepless night.

He woke up the next morning with a splitting headache and feeling thoroughly stressed; not only had he not slept properly, but he had also endured the surreal indignity of being poked with a stick in his dreams by none other than Mark Zuckerberg. Paul went to work feeling completely destroyed; he was reduced to spending the whole day hiding from Pamela because he could not think of a suitable excuse for his failure to come up with a solution. In the middle of the afternoon he started getting emails and SMS messages demanding to 'meet up' and 'touch base – urgently'. Unable to face any more of this relentless harassment, and tired of dodging about trying to avoid an encounter, he skulked off home, mumbling something to his secretary on his way out about a medical emergency. As he sat at home Paul reflected that he had a decision to make: either he had to find a way out or this was actually going to be the end of his career. He sat in his living room, surreptitiously watching his 14-year-old daughter, Alice, busy on the computer as ever, doubtless with her Facebook page.

After some minutes watching the girl's complete absorption, Paul decided to ask her how it worked. Alice looked at him with mock pity, groaned and said, 'I don't know what you mean. I'm busy. I've got things to do'. Paul paused, and then said quietly, 'This is serious. I do actually need you to tell me how this works'. Sensing something important was at stake, but still puzzled, Alice shrugged and began explaining what Facebook was and how it worked: she went through what she did on her own page and why she spent so much time there. Alice raced through this explanation far too quickly, and Paul was still a long way off understanding everything, but for the first time he started to see that there was a lot going on here. *So people formed groups did they? And got alerts by updates on their home pages? OK … So it's incredibly easy and straightforward for everyone to know what everyone else is doing, is it?*

Drawn in and mesmerised by his daughter's apparent natural affinity with the computer, for the next two hours Paul listened and watched intently, scribbling pages of notes. And as he did so, Alice felt that it was the first time her father was listening to her expertise and giving her so much in-depth attention. Alice started really opening up, explaining the technology and what excited her about it: the language, particular words; the funny stories of things that had happened; how people wrote stupid messages; and how things could get out of hand. Alice also enthusiastically demonstrated how she had been able to reconnect easily with some of her friends who had left the country.

By unburdening himself of his previous hostile views and listening with an open mind, Paul began to understand that this was not just another ephemeral technological toy waiting to be flung on the discard pile by people impatient for novelty; it really was a way of life, a way of being intimately connected with friends. And as he began to understand that simple truth, he also saw that it was not something outlandish and strange; it was just a new and better way of connecting, communicating and sharing – what people have always been doing, he thought ruefully to himself. So once Alice had finished the two-hour lecture, Paul put down his notepad, looked at his daugther and said, 'Here is my problem …', Alice frowned as she listened to her father's account of the company's troubles and replied, 'Well, I'm not sure I understand what all of that means, but here's what I've seen'. She quickly showed her father how people had arguments on Facebook and how groups formed around different topics; she found an example where somebody had got very angry because they had perceived a post to be offensive – and together they followed it through as the arguments had unfolded, with people coming back, responding and debating as the discussion flowed.

Alice told Paul about the more organised structure of Wikipedia too, at which point her dad smiled because *he* had finally grasped something about Wikipedia and how millions of volunteers could so effectively collaborate on a global project without being paid for it. By now Paul had accepted that Facebook really did have a central place in people's personal lives, but gradually he also began to see that all of this was not so different from the kind of *work* he normally did: 'So we're talking about communication, getting the right story to the right person and maybe explaining it differently if they don't get it at first', he asked Alice. 'Yeah, that's it, although I've never really thought about it before – I just do it without thinking', she announced breezily. Paul looked lovingly at his daughter and thought, 'Out of the mouth of babes …' indeed.

But despite his dawning recognition that there really was something of substance here, Paul still felt intimidated by the number of technological terms, gadgets and features that Alice had mentioned. He said, 'OK, but how do I actually solve the problem I've got?' His daughter looked at him, but with no idea of what to suggest she shrugged and told him, 'Just go online, start looking and start talking'. Paul still did not like the idea, but thought that the alternative was undoubtedly worse. He decided that based on what the company had done previously he should try to communicate directly with the person who had started the campaign. He returned to the Facebook group he had first visited a few days before, and researched some background information on the person. He found that she was upset and highly active, regularly blogging about technology and raging in particular that this one product that World Corp had launched did not function correctly. She had suffered because of this and it was, she argued, dangerous to portray the thing as something tried and tested; she had obviously tapped into a general sense of mistrust, and by talking about it relentlessly online a like-minded group of people had coalesced, seemingly out of nowhere.

Paul sat back and thought intently for a while; and then he decided to send her an email. He wrote:

> *I have read what you have been writing, and I've been looking at your blog. I understand where you are coming from. I also think that as a company it is our job to figure out how to deal with this. I cannot solve all the problems now, but what I can tell you is that I am going to do my best to try.*

He decided that because of everything he had heard about transparency and openness, there was no point whatsoever in pretending that this would remain private, so he posted the same message on Facebook. He created another account, put as much information on it about himself as he dared, and decided that he would respond to every single comment every single day until there was a favourable shift in the situation.

The next day he saw that there were hundreds of new comments about his response; some of them were quite angry but, to his surprise, a few of them were much more nuanced. Many people seemed pleased simply because there had actually been any response at all from someone at the company. Paul also got a response from the main driver, who seemed to have lost a little, if not much, of her fire:

> *I still completely disagree with you. I think your company is being outrageous and irresponsible ... but I appreciate the fact that you sent me that note.*

Encouraged by the fact that he wasn't completely drowning in online vitriol, and had even slightly disarmed the person behind the whole thing, Paul then started looking at World Corp's internal processes, trying to identify what the company could do and what it should do better. He knew that according to protocol he should have cleared this with the legal department and numerous levels of upper management, but he also knew that if he did not get some kind of result soon he would probably get fired in the next round of restructuring. As he worked steadily to try to find a solution, he looked at what the company had done and said when dealing with similar problems that had arisen in the past. It turned out that there was actually a great deal of information freely available, but no one – either in the company itself or from among the massed armies of online critics – had bothered to look. Rather than keeping this to himself, Paul began sending links to these previous press releases to people in the Facebook group, patiently explaining to them that:

> *This is what we tried to do before; it may not have been good enough, but what I can tell you is that I have made sure that we are on to this, that we have made this a priority.*

The majority of the feedback remained negative, but slowly a more rational, coherent and informed discussion began to emerge – it was critical, but at least there was a new sense of people trying to openly and honestly work through a difficult problem. Inspired by seeing this, Paul then created a thread of his own on the Facebook page by openly inviting people to answer the simple question: 'How can we find a solution to this situation?' He found that numerous people – colleagues from within the company as well as some of those who were leading the campaign against it – were eager to join in. Paul kept probing away, constantly encouraging people to submit ideas, asking, 'So, what else could we do? How can we address this in a way that ensures we avoid these problems in the future?' He was amazed to find some good ideas popping up in this new discussion, and gradually the whole campaign against the company became less aggressive. Paul carefully studied what was said, took it all in and kept detailed notes of events as they progressed and unfolded. He didn't really know why – he just felt that the information might prove useful sometime in the future. Most importantly, he began to feel that there *was* a way out and that he had found it; it was now just a matter of leading people along the right path.

Others, however, remained to be convinced. Paul's online initiative had caused quite a stir in the company, and word of what was going on inevitably reached Pamela. Eventually Paul got the email he had been expecting, written with her usual refined sense of economy: 'My office. NOW.' Paul opened the door feeling quite confident, but then shrank somewhat when he found Pamela looking volcanic with rage. She growled:

> *What's all this I've heard about you communicating on Facebook with the idiots who have been criticising us? Exactly how does that fit our corporate guidelines? Have you checked it with legal?*

Paul saw that she had a long list of points on a piece of paper in front of her – no doubt of all the things that he had not done correctly. 'It seems to me', she went on in a ferocious tone that compelled his silence, 'that you have broken at least ten of our guidelines, and I do not remember telling you to go ahead and do any of these things without checking with me'. By now Paul was feeling sick, but he *knew* that he had been doing something that was working. He tried to explain and defend himself, suggesting that maybe these 'idiots' had a point – it was just hidden inside all of their rage. At this, Pamela just stared at him. Eventually she said, slowly and quietly:

> *I'll be discussing this with management, and I'll be getting back to you later on this week. In the meantime, just try not to make things worse. You've started this and you can't very well stop it, but be damn careful about what else you write. And keep me posted on everything.*

Paul went back to his office having decided that he was now well on the way to getting fired; but rather than adopt the customary role of bitter and disgruntled soon-to-be ex-employee, he surprised himself by thinking, no, I won't do that: *I'll carry on in the time I have left and go out gracefully, having tried my best to the very end.* So for the rest of that day and the rest of the week he diligently continued to do as he had done before, reaching out to even the most hostile critics, trying to defuse their anger by candidly explaining things, suggesting ideas and seeking their views; but, ever mindful of his boss's ferocious temper, he was cautious not to write anything that might cause further trouble.

The following week – having surprisingly heard nothing further from Pamela – Paul was astonished, and then horrified, to receive an email from no less than the president of the company. It read, 'Need to talk. Call'. The Pamela School of Email Etiquette, he noted wryly. Surely he doesn't even know I exist, Paul thought, but then the ghastly truth dawned on him: 'Well', he said to himself aloud, 'this is it. I've reached the end, all right. I may as well start clearing my desk'. After delaying for as long as he possibly could, Paul picked up the phone, literally shaking, and immediately got put through to the president, who greeted him with a warm and booming 'Howdy Paul'. The next 15 minutes were slightly surreal as the president of World Corp happily rattled along, telling Paul that he had seen his work and heard great things about how it really was changing the way the company was perceived online. He wanted to have Paul oversee an exciting project to further change the company's culture; this had been on the agenda for some time – he may even have heard a few rumours.

Paul smiled. He felt excited and motivated. He knew this would be a massive challenge for him. He also knew that he was able to learn again, and that with that in mind it would probably be a great ride. He agreed, and put the phone down. As he walked back home that evening he felt a surge of confidence and energy – not because he felt he had achieved something, but because he felt ready to learn, to change and shift. He had embraced his unpredictable future and was going to give it his best shot.

Index

Xbox 61

Yammer (closed version of
    Facebook) 95, 116
'Young Achievers Award' 37
YouTube 82–3, 99, 108–9, 115,
    131, 134–5, 138, 142

YouTube channel 131
YouTube video 82

ZeitgeistNet *see* ZN
ZN 37–8, 40, 54–6, 95, 138
Zuckerberg, Mark 17, 110, 144

If you have found this book useful you may be interested in other titles from Gower

Business Wargaming
Securing Corporate Value
Daniel F. Oriesek and Jan Oliver Schwarz
Hardback: 978-0-566-08837-7
e-book: 978-0-7546-9096-2

Communicating Strategy
Phil Jones
Paperback: 978-0-566-08810-0
e-book: 978-0-7546-8288-2

Enterprise 2.0
**How Social Software Will Change
the Future of Work**
Niall Cook
Hardback: 978-0-566-08800-1

Game Theory in Management
**Modelling Business Decisions
and their Consequences**
Michael Hatfield
Hardback: 978-1-4094-4241-7
e-book: 978-1-4094-4242-4

Global HR
Challenges Facing the Function
Peter Reilly and Tony Williams
Hardback: 978-1-4094-0278-7
e-book: 978-1-4094-0279-4

GOWER

Human Resources or Human Capital?
Managing People as Assets
Andrew Mayo
Hardback: 978-1-4094-2285-3
e-book: 978-1-4094-2286-0

Plan for the Planet
A Business Plan for a Sustainable World
Ian Chambers and John Humble
Hardback: 978-1-4094-4589-0
e-book: 978-1-4094-0682-2

The Changing MO of the CMO
How the Convergence of Brand and
Reputation is Affecting Marketers
MaryLee Sachs
Hardback: 978-1-4094-2315-7
e-book: 978-1-4094-2316-4

The Focused Organization
How Concentrating on a Few Key Initiatives
Can Dramatically Improve Strategy Execution
Antonio Nieto-Rodriguez
Hardback: 978-1-4094-2566-3
e-book: 978-1-4094-2567-0

Visit **www.gowerpublishing.com** and

- search the entire catalogue of Gower books in print
- order titles online at 10% discount
- take advantage of special offers
- sign up for our monthly e-mail update service
- download free sample chapters
  from all recent titles
- download or order our catalogue